The Great Themes of the Qur'an

The Great Themes of the Qur'an

Jacques Jomier

SCM PRESS LTD

Translated by Zoe Hersov from the French *Les grands thèmes du Coran*, published 1978 by Éditions Le Centurion, Paris.

0 334 02714 4

First published 1997 by
SCM Press Ltd
9–17 St Albans Place London N1 0NX

Typeset at The Spartan Press Ltd
Lymington, Hants
and printed in Great Britain by
Biddles Ltd, Guildford and King's Lynn

Contents

Contents

Translator's Note

In order to make this work more accessible, I have not used diacritical marks in the transliteration of Arabic words except in the case of terms in italics. The spelling of names and places follows current practice.

The English renderings of the Qur'anic texts are mainly based on A. J. Arberry, *The Koran Interpreted*, London: Allen and Unwin 1995. Also consulted were M. M. Pickthall, *The Meaning of the Glorious Qur'an*, New York: New American Library and Mentor books, n.d.; A. Yusuf Ali, *The Holy Qur'an*, Dar al-Arabia 1965; Muhammad Asad, *The Message of the Qur'an*, Gibraltar: Dar al-Andalus 1984; J. M. Rodwell, *The Koran*, London: J. M. Dent 1950; Richard Bell, *The Qur'an. Translated with a Critical Rearrangement of the Surahs* (2 vols), Edinburgh: T. and T. Clark 1937–1939; and N. J. Dawood, *The Koran*, Harmondsworth: Penguin Books 1980.

The aim has been to remain as faithful as possible to the Arabic while at the same time attempting to convey something of the haunting beauty of the original.

Introduction

The following pages have been written at the request of some people who were eager to understand the Qur'an. They were not Muslims and their first encounter with the text had completely daunted them. The references to historical facts and events little known outside Islam, the style, the religious perceptions and even the values, that are at once so familiar and so alien to someone with a background in Western culture, all conspire to make the Qur'an an impenetrable, closed book. And yet these same people, all of whom live in the Muslim world, work with Muslims and would like to understand and be on friendly terms with them, were well aware of the fact that the Qur'an lies at the heart of Islam. They knew that it could even be said that Islam is the Qur'an, since the veneration in which it is held, the reading of the text and deeply reverent meditation on it, have made a profound impression on the general climate as well as on the individual outlook of the faithful. So, in spite of the difficulties they encountered, they persevered with their project. Hence this request.

A presentation of some of the great themes developed in the Qur'an seemed to be the simplest way to help them. By taking selected passages, underlining the literary devices and drawing attention to both the religious ideas and the way in which they are expressed, we will enable readers to become familiar with the text. This is a first step. Later more extensive personal reading, as well as a better understanding of life and customs in the Muslim world, can complete this introduction. Without such a foundation, the enterprise could all too easily come to nothing. Subsequent experience and personal contacts, useful as they may be, will bear fruit only if sustained by the minimum general knowledge necessary for an initial understanding of the text.

At the same time this presentation is intended to be accessible to those whom life has placed in contact with Muslims, in Europe or elsewhere, and who merely seek preliminary information on a subject that is completely new to them. There are numerous introductions to Islam: a review of the great Qur'anic themes may prove useful to complement them.

Before the present work was written, it was explored and discussed in two or three closed groups and many of the observations it contains were suggested by this experience. Each chapter begins with a survey designed to place the theme to be studied in the light of some important verses. We then turn to the Qur'an itself. A selected text is given in an English translation and accompanied by a commentary. If necessary, attention is drawn to other passages in the Qur'an that view the subject from the same or a similar angle.

We must also bear in mind a question of vocabulary. While Christians use the word gospel to describe both the original Greek text and the many versions in other languages, attaching the greatest importance to the essential ideas and message, Muslims regard only the Arabic version of the Qur'an as truly sacred. Certainly there are translations of the Qur'an in various languages, but normally only Arabic is used in liturgical recitations. Translations are authorized in order to make the 'ideas' of the Qur'an known to the faithful, when ignorance of Arabic would prevent a fruitful reading of the original text. But the sacred character of the Arabic language and the scrupulous respect for the smallest letter accord a unique place to the Arabic original.

Above all we shall look for the human and religious base that underlies the text and is at the root of the personal relation between the Muslim and his Creator. The Qur'an returns again and again to certain fundamental truths or essential points of doctrine, affirming them with such insistence that no one can be misled. However, in other places, it confines itself to suggestion, making perception and appreciation of the nuances a more delicate matter. In such cases, the commentators often illustrate the text with the general teaching of the Qur'an, rediscovering once again in the obscure passages what is said elsewhere in clearly formulated pronouncements (cf. Qur'an 3,7: 'He it is who has sent down to thee the Book; in it are verses clear that are the Essence of the Book – and others allegorical . . . '). All we can do then is to try very humbly to discern what our Muslim brothers see in the passage concerned. We will succeed only if we are prepared to listen to them tactfully, without taking their positions as hard and fast, knowing that there are different tendencies among them that are capable of development.

In conclusion, attention must be drawn to another important fact. The role of the Qur'an in the history of Islam and the life of the community does not depend solely on its teaching, that is on its intellectual aspect, but also on the extraordinary impact it has on the emotional consciousness of all Muslims. The veneration that surrounds it, observed by the faithful from early childhood; the holy terror of making a mistake by mispronouncing the smallest letter, and the immediate, almost brutal, reaction of those around if ever such an error occurs; the ritual purity demanded of those who touch it; the chanting of its verses on the most moving occasions in family and social life as well as at crises in the nation's history; the endless liturgical recitations; the tension of the crowd that listens and expresses its admiration for the virtuosity of the reciter as much as for the meaning itself; the continual repetition of certain verses in ritual prayer; the use of entire phrases as decorative motifs in the most magnificent monuments of Islamic art; the masterpieces of calligraphy that it has produced; the appeal to its authority to end all discussion; the rejection of the slightest doubt, however well-formulated, not only in the case of the Qur'an but also, in practice, when it comes to many of the traditional interpretations; the continual affirmation of its miraculous character and its inimitable qualities, so that it alone offers a solution to the gravest problems in every time and place; the unfailing acceptance of the text as the supreme criterion of literary aesthetics ... all this creates an atmosphere that is difficult for the non-Muslim to imagine. Analogies could perhaps be found in the emotions inspired in a Christian by the memory of family Christmases, or by the sound of a Bach organ fugue in the half-light of a quiet church, or even in the sonorous strains of a national anthem after victory. It is not only the intellect that is affected but all the fibres of one's being. The Qur'an itself pictures the power that it exerts when it describes how, during its recitation, the skin reacts under a kind of religious spell:

'God has sent down the fairest discourse as a Book, consistent with itself, teaching by repetition, whereat shiver the skins of those who fear their Lord; then do their skins and their hearts soften at the remembrance of God' (Qur'an 39. 23).

I

What is the Qur'an?

For the Muslim, the Qur'an is a book whose author is God Himself. According to the teachings of Islam, God created the entire universe, then the angels, and then mankind in the person of Adam and his wife. The history of humanity began with the disobedience of the first couple and their expulsion from the earthly paradise. But God did not abandon them and promised to guide them by the prophets.

Some of the prophets brought men sacred books from God, the best known being the Torah, the Psalms and the Gospel. These books were misused and falsified, so God finally sent Muhammad with the Qur'an and He promised to ensure that the text of this last book would never be corrupted. For the Muslim, the Qur'an simply repeats the religious teaching of the previous scriptures, setting out once again the eternal doctrine that was already known to Adam in its entirety. Therefore the Qur'an is, for him, an encyclopedia that contains the essence of the revelations made to the prophets, preserving them so perfectly that the reader has no need to have recourse to other sacred books. All the essential points, in every aspect, are given to him in the Qur'an.

The Muslim, therefore, regards the Qur'an as the most sacred object on earth, God's supreme gift to humanity. This position entails certain consequences that will determine our attitude.

The rules of etiquette

In the Muslim world, there is a whole body of literature

concerned with how to treat an Arabic copy of the Qur'an. The book must not be handled casually; it must not be left lying around. If there are other books, the Muslim always places the Qur'an on the top of the pile. To put anything above it would show lack of respect. There are places where it cannot be taken and others where it is not taken out of its case. It is not done to smoke or eat when reading it. While some Muslims may at times read it on a train or tram, this would be repugnant to others for reasons of ritual purity. In the homes of pious Muslims, a copy often lies open in a place of honour in the middle of a display cabinet or in a glass-fronted bookcase. And in Cairo, a custom developed for cars to feature a box containing a copy of the Qur'an which was prominently displayed on the dashboard or in the back of the car.

How does a Muslim experience the Qur'an?

A Muslim learns to respect the Qur'an from his earliest years. Two examples will give some idea of the depth of feeling it arouses.

In a conversation one day, a Muslim woman from the Middle East recalled what the Qur'an had meant to her in childhood. She used to see her father reading it with reverence and meditating on it. Sometimes, in the month of Ramadan, there was a more formal ceremony at the house and a professional reciter, a specialist sheikh, came to chant verses in a simple, haunting melody. If the book was dropped by mistake, it was picked up at once, wiped and the cover was kissed. It was not cleaned with an ordinary duster: one always chose a spotless cloth that had never been used for this purpose.

The second example dates from 1977, when President Anwar Sadat, speaking to members of a Congress of 'Ulama', Muslim jurists from all over the world who had gathered for a kind of synod in Cairo, described the part religion had played in his life. As a child in the village, he had learnt whole pages of the Qur'an by heart and certain verses remained engraved on his memory:

he never ceased to find strength in them throughout his life. For instance, there is this verse on the nearness of God that he repeated before delegates from forty-five Muslim countries:

> 'And when My servants question thee concerning Me – lo, I am near to answer the call of the caller, when he calls to Me' (Qur'an 2. 186).

And later, when he had become an officer and was arrested for plotting against the English occupying forces with the aim of liberating Egypt, he spent long hours meditating on the Qur'an in his prison cell, near the Cairo fortress.

Marks of respect for the book itself and meditation on verses that are remembered and that sustain the faithful in their relationship with God are two aspects that are very characteristic of the attitude of the Muslim towards the Qur'an.

A simple teaching

The Qur'an is first and foremost a book of exhortations, practical advice and at times legislation. It contains a great many felicitous phrases, similar to maxims, that the faithful memorize. Some of them serve as ejaculatory prayers.

Its teaching is simple, revolving around certain central ideas that it repeats insistently so that they are imprinted on the mind and especially the heart of believers, like the main themes of a symphony which recur at given times. For example, God is all-powerful; He is the sole creator, infinitely good and forgiving. All that man has is a gift and grace from God. Men are good and bad; God guides them by His messengers and His Books. All the communities that preceded Islam possessed the truth for a time. Then they fell away and were unfaithful to their vocation, so that today Islam alone is the criterion of all truth. The world has been entrusted to the Muslim community to reign peacefully, but if need be by war; this is the Law of God. All men will die, and then one day God will raise, judge and punish them for their conduct during their earthly life. Those who worship several gods or who oppose the Messengers of the one God will be severely punished, but the good will enjoy everlasting bliss. Therefore man must strive to please God in whose sight he always lives, to obey Him and follow His messengers obediently, to be content with his lot, give thanks, bear affliction, observe the law, and so on.

The Qur'an thus contains a core of assertions that it repeats over and over again. The rest is allusive, remaining deliberately vague so as not to distract the attention.

How the collection of the Qur'anic texts was formed

Copies of the Qur'an today contain a text that has been carefully fixed. It is a collection made of up a hundred and fourteen chapters of unequal length, divided into verses: in the Arabic text, the verses end in a sort of rhyme, or at least assonance, that remains the same for a number of refrains. These chapters are called in Arabic 'suras', a word that has been adopted in many English books on Islam. The first chapter that serves as an opening of the book (hence its name, the *Fātiḥa*) is a prayer that Muslims constantly repeat and that plays an even more important part in their liturgy than the Lord's Prayer does in Christian services. This is the text:

'In the name of God, the Merciful, the Compassionate

Praise be to God, the Lord of the Worlds,
The Merciful, the Compassionate,
The Master of the Day of Judgment.
Thee only do we worship; to Thee alone do we call for help.
Guide us in the straight path,
The path of those whom Thou hast blessed,
Not of those against whom Thou art wrathful,
Nor of those who go astray. Amen.'

The chapters that follow are arranged in general in order of decreasing length. Thus the second chapter, or sura, has 286 verses, while the last ones in the book have between 3 and 6.

The text of the Qur'an is made up of a series of oracles proclaimed by Muhammad in the name of God, which all Muslims regard as the very word of God. These oracles were memorized by those who heard them and subsequently set down in writing, initially on a variety of fragmentary objects. The first attempt to collect them in a single book took place a year or two after the death of Muhammad, when a hard military campaign in central Arabia had brought about the death of many of the original Companions. To put a complete version of the Qur'an into writing entailed preserving all the passages hitherto confined to the memory of mortals destined to die.

The work was resumed fifteen or twenty years later, at the order of the Caliph 'Uthman (who reigned from 644 to 656); it resulted in the first official recension of the Book and representative copies were sent to the great military capitals of the empire. The Arabic script then in usage was still rather like shorthand, less accurate than the present script and open to ambiguous interpretations. The orthography was slowly perfected and two centuries later the text was definitively established. There were a few variant readings arising from schools in different countries; but these variants did not affect the underlying meaning of the text. Thus orthodox Islam officially admits a certain number of canonical readings (seven, ten or fourteen, according to opinion). In addition, at the beginning of Islam, there were distinctive ways of reading particular verses that were favoured by certain Companions. The commentators of the Qur'an sometimes cite these divergent opinions.

The variant collections have left their trace on some translations. Furthermore, since the break in the verses was not made in exactly the same way in all the schools, there is a resulting discrepancy in the numbering found in the translated editions.

The old translations by orientalists use the numbering of the readings of the Qur'an formerly observed in North Africa. Today there is a tendency to adopt the one followed by the official Cairo editions. Some translations indicate both. I shall give only the Cairo version.

Final remarks

The actual compilation of the Qur'anic oracles was the work of an official commission appointed by the caliphs. Due to the fragmentary nature of the texts to be collected, the final work presents a mosaic of passages arranged in a certain order, as far as possible grouping texts of the same period in the same sura. However, Muslims firmly adhere to the actual order of the Arabic version that the jurists attribute to the will of God.

On the other hand, the title of each sura was given later and is not regarded as revealed. In general it is taken from the contents of the sura. Thus the sura called 'The Bee' (Sura 16) refers at some point to those insects; the one called 'Mary' (Sura 19) devotes more than twenty verses to Mary and Jesus. Some suras can have different titles according to the traditions: thus the sura of 'The Night Journey' (Sura 17) is also called 'The Children of Israel'.

In conclusion, mention should be made of the care with which Muslims have sought to recover the chronological order of the suras, and even at times the antiquity of some important verse. There are traditional lists that state that one sura was revealed after another, and so on, thus setting out two groups: those dating from Mecca, before the Hijra in 622, and those from Medina, after the Hijra. The reason for the interest taken in these dates is mainly legal. As certain points of law unfolded during the twenty years of Muhammad's ministry, it is useful to know which was the final form of the law. Fermented drinks were permitted at the beginning, then discouraged and finally forbidden. The fact that the verse formally forbidding these drinks is later than those that permit them is advanced by the jurists to justify their interpretation.

Furthermore, the reader will discern some differences of style and atmosphere between the oldest suras on the Last Judgment, with their breathless, impassioned passages, and the more recent ones, with a slower rhythm, that often contain long, legal expositions.

2

Mecca and the Early Days of Islam

The Qur'an is based on ordinary life as it was lived by men in the Hijaz when Islam emerged, and during the preceding decades. It focuses on a very limited number of events, chosen for their importance or their evocative power, and it links these events directly to God. To use the Qur'an solely as a source of information about the life of that period is not very fruitful. Admittedly the facts are there. But having uncovered them, it is wiser to concentrate attention on the action of God.

For example, the text seeks to show that God protected the city of Mecca against assailants, sustained it and shielded it from fear, as He also protected Muhammad and entrusted him with revelation. Thus God is described as the Lord who is very powerful and good to those who are closely or remotely touched by prophecy and who submit obediently to His guidance. Then comes the attitude that is demanded, explicitly or implicitly, from man in return.

The expedition mounted against the Ka'ba; Meccan commerce

'Hast thou not seen how thy Lord dealt with the Army of the Elephant? Did He not bring their stratagem to naught? And sent against them flocks of birds, which pelted them with stones of baked clay, and made them like stubble eaten down' (Qur'an 105. 1–5).

'For the security of the Quraysh, their security in the winter and summer caravan! So let them worship the Lord of this House who has fed them against hunger, and made them safe from fear' (Qur'an 106. 1–4).

We find here a formula that is frequently employed in the Qur'an: 'Hast thou not seen how?' It is an invitation to recall an act in the past: this act took place too long ago for any of the listeners to have witnessed it, but its lesson is presented as still relevant. The effect of the style is to attract attention with the striking use of 'see' in order to emphasize the certainty. A lesson is to be learned about a well-defined fact and the lesson is made clear in advance. It is like an exercise under the direction of a teacher who dwells neither on the historical aspect of the event, nor on a critical analysis of the facts. The teacher presents the lesson and demands the listener's assent. It is tantamount to saying: did God, or did He not, protect the people of Mecca against their aggressors? To a question posed in this way, the faithful can only reply in the affirmative. Hence it is also a statement of the total dependence of man on God who is all-powerful and infinitely good.

The first text comes from Sura 105, the sura called The Elephant. It describes an expedition that was mounted against the Hijaz by Abraha, viceroy of the Yemen, on behalf of the Negus, towards the middle of the sixth century, therefore less than a hundred years before Islam. Inscriptions refer to an expedition of this kind, but it took place well before the birth of Muhammad, whereas here the commentators say that it concerns an expedition in the same year as his birth. An elephant that was included in the army caught the people's imagination, hence the name Army of the Elephant that was given to the expeditionary force. Muslim hagiography reports that the column was checked by an unusual kind of bombardment. Birds, carrying stones, hurled them at the assailants, who fled in disorder.

The details given are very sparse. The lesson is that God miraculously protects Mecca and its inhabitants, repels attacks and brings victory. The interest of this sura is to show the Muslims' faith in the victory that God gives His own. To be noted, too, is the interrogative style that keeps the audience on their toes.

The absence of detail has allowed commentators to embellish the story richly. Some modern writers interpret the stones as microbes. The defeat could thus be attributed to an epidemic. This example illustrates the evocative power of phrases, at first sight quite general but gradually enriched and transformed by memory and emotion. For, in reality, this is not intended to be a history lesson. On the contrary, all the emphasis is on a practical conclusion, a clear-cut attitude demanded of man. The conclusion may be implicit, as in the call for gratitude (Sura 105), or explicit, like the order to worship the Lord of the Ka'ba (Sura 106).

Sura 106 mentions the Quraysh, the tribe to which the people of Mecca, and consequently Muhammad and the first Muslims, all belonged. It describes the mercantile activity of the population. Mecca was, in fact, an important commercial centre on a trade route extending from India to the Mediterranean sea. Other routes linked the two zones, one traversing the Red Sea and Egypt, the other the Arabian-Persian Gulf and the Euphrates. The wars between Byzantium and Persia that had gone on for decades and were at their height at the time Muhammad began to preach undoubtedly had repercussions on the Meccan trade. In 610, Muhammad had his first visions. There followed two or three years when he experienced nothing and then it all began again in 612, only two years before the capture of Jerusalem by the Persians in 614. The war may also have affected trade in Syria.

Once a year in winter, the Meccans went in a quasi-official caravan (not to mention other private journeys) to Aden, in South Arabia. Their aim was to seek the merchandise deposited there by ships carried by the seasonal winter winds from India. In actual fact it is at this time of year that winds regularly blow from India towards Arabia. The Meccans then brought the goods back to Mecca before going to the Mediterranean basin (to Busra in Syria, Gaza or Lower Egypt) to trade. There was also the summer caravan. The commentators remark that winter was much more favourable for travel in the torrid regions of the south, while in summer the temperature in Syria was quite bearable.

The benefits of commerce are attributed to God, the Lord of the temple of the Ka'ba. This title given to God (Allah in Arabic) implicitly assumes that the Arabs recognize God's sovereignty over the 'associates' they ascribe to him. It is He who gives food (thanks to trade) and security, since the territory of Mecca was sacred. This meant that all hostility was absolutely forbidden there by ancient Arab custom. So let the Quraysh worship the Lord of the Ka'ba. This is a call for grateful, trusting worship. There is much evidence of a similar attitude in the Old Testament.

Mecca's commercial aspect has been emphasized in Marxist materialist explanations of the origins of Islam. It was certainly a factor but, for one thing, we know very little about the actual circumstances of this trade and, besides, there are many other elements that need to be considered.

What does the reference to the security of the Quraysh mean? Does it relate to the defence of Mecca against the attack of the Army of the Elephant, or to the successful conclusion of commercial transactions? This security was soon to be disrupted by the preaching of Muhammad, only to return in the end at the time of the triumph of Islam.

The childhood and youth of Muhammad

'In the name of God, the Merciful, the Compassionate

By the morning light, and by the fall of night! Thy Lord has not forsaken thee, nor does He hate thee. And surely the Last shall be better for thee than the First. Thy Lord shall give thee, and thou shalt be satisfied. Did He not find thee an orphan, and shelter thee? Did He not find thee wandering, and guide thee? Did He not find thee needy, and enrich thee? So as for the orphan, do not oppress him, and as for the beggar, chide him not away; and as for thy Lord's bounty, proclaim it' (Qur'an 93. 1–11).

'In the name of God, the Merciful, the Compassionate

Did We not expand thy breast for thee and lift from thee thy burden, the burden that weighed down thy back? Did We not exalt thy fame? So truly with hardship comes ease, truly with hardship comes ease. So when thou art free, labour, and seek thy Lord with fervour' (Qur'an 94. 1–8).

These very short chapters allude to the childhood and youth of Muhammad in order to emphasize God's protection of him. We will take note of three words in Sura 93, each one preceded by a parallel grammatical construction ['Did He not find thee . . . ']: orphan, wandering and poor.

Orphan, for Muhammad never knew his father 'Abdallah, who died on a journey when his wife Amina was with child. She, in turn, died when her son was six years old; and Muhammad's grandfather passed away two years later. So, at the age of eight, he was taken in by his uncle Abu Talib, who brought him up and then bravely protected him from all those who were set against him.

What does the word wandering mean? The commentators have wondered about it because in the Qur'an this term is always reserved for those who have no knowledge of Islam and are not on the straight path. How then can a prophet, endowed with all the qualities that title entails, be described as wandering? The Qur'an commentary of Fakhr al-Din al-Razi (died in 1210) offers twenty different explanations of the word 'wandering', a proof of the complexity of the question for Muslims. A few scholars are of the opinion that Muhammad, from his birth to his call, adhered to the paganism of his people, but the body of jurists cannot admit that he was ever for a single moment anything but a monotheist. Others suggest that the word refers to a day when, at the age of three, he lost his way in the town of Mecca and was restored to his parents by a Christian first cousin of his future wife, Khadija. Or else that the caravan to which he was attached got lost in the desert one day. The word can also be taken to express his perplexity at the beginning after his first dream. We learn from this example that the very conciseness of the Qur'an gives the style an elliptical quality that arrests the reader, whose view of the word is coloured by his own rich emotions and memories. It is not a matter of knowing exactly how Muhammad could be wandering, but only of placing his memory in an atmosphere surrounded by the grace and goodness of God and enhancing his prestige by his unique relationship with God.

We note too that there is no account of Muhammad's religious practice before Islam. There were monotheists living in Mecca. Two first cousins of Muhammad's wife, Khadija, were Christians and one of them, Waraqa ibn Nawfal, possessed copies of the holy books. The texts, Qur'anic and otherwise, say almost nothing about their relationship. It is the same with the alternation of hardship and ease (Sura 94, verses 5 and 6). Repeating this maxim twice, the text recalls the vicissitudes of life in generalities that are self-evident but very necessary to remember if one is to keep one's spirits up in times of trial.

Muhammad's poverty derived from his position as an orphan. Early in life, he had to go into trade in the service of a wealthy widow, Khadija, whom he then married despite the difference in age. It is said that she was fifteen years older than he was.

Orphan, wandering, poor, ... these three words merely describe reality in very general terms that can support any number of possible details: they move the reader or listener by the pity they arouse. In this way the Qur'an tends to speak of facts or stories the details of which are already known to listeners and concentrates all the interest on the lesson to be learned.

The following sura (Sura 94) continues the preceding one, pointing once again to the grace of God who exalted Muhammad. The expression 'expand thy breast' has given rise to numerous legends about the angel who opened Muhammad's chest and washed his heart before replacing it. The words burden and fame remain very general. But the commandments are precise: help the weak, pray, recount the Lord's blessings. Prayer, moreover, is characteristic of Islam; at the beginning, in the years in Mecca, night-vigils were common. In Medina, the atmosphere and demands of battle reduced their frequency and duration.

We notice an allusion to the afterlife. For from the beginning of the preaching, the Qur'anic appeals were centred on the two poles of the Unity of God and the Last Things (resurrection, judgment, heaven and hell). We observe too the place that the person of Muhammad occupies in these texts and the support they provide for devotion to him.

In short, these two suras describe both the blessings of God, a theme to which the Qur'an so often returns, and the form of grace that consists in guiding men, another idea that appears again and again in the Qur'an.

The style here is very clear. For emphasis it employs repetition, at the same time knowing how to vary the form. The word 'find' recurs three times but [in the Arabic original] is used the first time in the interrogative and the other times in the affirmative:

'Did He not find thee an orphan?' (Qur'an 93. 6).

The narrative also involves a progression. Starting with a particular fact, Muhammad's situation, the text points at once to the attitude of God. Then the conclusion is drawn, with a view either to social action or to the praise of God. In both cases the listener's mind is led to the Lord. And it is with the thought of the Lord that the whole passage comes to rest, inducing silence and contemplation.

The description of such good fortune always excites popular admiration: this is a fact well known to storytellers, who hold their audience when they rescue their hero from misfortune, guide and enrich him ... The glamour of success and prosperity ... especially when they make amends for poverty or poignant loneliness. The commandments or the reflections about God take on the appearance of obvious fact after the style has prepared the ground. There is no discussion: the Qur'an wins the audience's support.

Finally, we note the human motives to which the text appeals: first of all, pity, which is often found, but there is tenderness, too, which is rarer; also the description of success and power – the view of the future with God who 'guides' – and above all, a profound sense of the presence of God.

Muhammad's call

'Recite: In the name of thy Lord who created, created man from a blood-clot. Recite: for thy Lord is Most Generous, who taught by the pen, taught man what he knew not' (Qur'an 96. 1–5).

The entire Muslim tradition is unanimous that these five verses constitute the call of Muhammad, the announcement of his mission.

As noted above, we know nothing at all about the relations between Muhammad and the monotheists in Mecca, before and in the early days of Islam. The only thing we do know is that (perhaps every year, but certainly that year) he went to make a retreat in a cave in Mount Hira, near Mecca. Was this motivated by a private inspiration? Or was it the practice of certain monotheist groups? It is hard to know.

It was during one such retreat, around the year 610, when he was about forty years old, that he had a dream or, to use the terms employed by Bukhari, a true vision in his sleep. According to this tradition, the angel came and said to him: 'Read!' 'I cannot read,' answered Muhammad. The angel squeezed him and then released him and repeated the order, which was once again followed by the same sequence of actions. Finally the angel recited the five verses and Muhammad, terribly distressed, hastened back to Mecca and took refuge in Khadija's arms, in fear and trembling. She wrapped him in a cloak or blanket to warm him and events took their course ... In sum, these five verses proclaim the creation of man by God (and his reproduction by procreation, as evoked by the term 'blood-clot'), and then declare that God taught man.

The verses are advanced by Muslims when they want to affirm the place of learning and reading in Islam. In fact, the text proclaims yet again that man owes everything to the generosity of God, the all-powerful Creator, knowledge and writing as well as life.

Muslim tradition goes into fairly crude detail when it reports how Khadija encouraged her husband. When he returned to the house, having seen the angel again, Khadija embraced him in an uninhibited fashion permitted only by conjugal intimacy. The angel disappeared: this was a good sign, for a devil would not have shown the same sense of modesty and would have stayed. Then, alone (or, according to another tradition, with her husband), she went to consult her first cousin Waraqa ibn Nawfal, the most important Christian in Mecca. He reassured her and announced that Muhammad was the prophet of this *umma*, that is, 'nation' (is the word Arab to be inferred?). These Muslim sources also imply that Waraqa ibn Nawfal saw Muhammad as a long-awaited prophet. If the account is authentic, this man must have belonged to a sect like the one that gave rise to the pseudo-Clementine literature. Such sects, which had much in common with both Judaism and Christianity, taught that an eternal prophet would return periodically to the world.

For two or three years, nothing more happened. Finally in 612, the phenomena resumed and from that time Muhammad began to proclaim the oracles that later, collected in a single volume, would form the Qur'an. The proclamation took place, piecemeal, in the course of the next twenty years until 632, the date of Muhammad's death.

The word 'Read!', which can also mean 'Recite', comes from an old Semitic root found in the word Qur'an. Qur'an means 'recitation' and, in a secondary sense, 'sacred text that is recited'. This is exactly the same meaning today of the Syriac word with the same structure, *qeryānā*: a term signifying, in the Maronite rite, the ritual 'readings' of the office or Mass, that is, the sacred texts to be read or recited.

Two manifestations of a superhuman being

In the name of God, the Merciful, the Compassionate

By the Star when it sets, your companion is not astray, nor is deceived, neither does he speak out of his own desire. This is naught but a revelation revealed, one terrible in power taught it him, very strong; he stood poised, upon the high horizon, then drew near and came down till he was two bows'-length away, or nearer, and He revealed to His servant what He revealed. His heart lied not of what he saw. What, will you dispute with him as to what he saw? Indeed, he saw him another time by the Lote-tree of the Boundary, near which is the Garden of Abode, when there covered the Lote-tree that which covered it. His eye swerved not, nor did it stray. Indeed, he saw one of the greatest signs of his Lord' (Qur'an, Sura 53, The Star, 1–18).

The commentators are unanimous that this passage concerns

Muhammad's misson and describes the way revelation came to him.

The text is later than the preceding five verses. It dates from the time when the preaching of Islam began to arouse criticism and opposition. In fact the Qur'an contains a number of passages relating to these controversies (for example, Qur'an 69. 38–52; 25. 4–10; 16.102–103, etc.).

The sura begins with an oath that invokes natural phenomena. The device is common in the earliest suras. Here the subject is the Star; in Sura 93, it was morning and night. Was this the custom of soothsayers in pre-Islamic Arabia when they pronounced their oracles? Or is it the echo of an attested practice of certain Christian baptist sects whose teaching has been preserved for us in a literature known as 'pseudo-Clementine', that is, attributed to Clement of Rome? It is impossible to say.

The commentators of the Qur'an remark that these oaths are intended to magnify the subject of the appeal. It is a way of calling attention to the grandeur of created things and thus of their Creator to whom they owe everything.

The text describes two manifestations of a superior being: is it God Himself? Or is it Gabriel, the angel of revelation? The commentators mention the two possibilities, perhaps laying more stress on the second, the apparition of the angel Gabriel.

We find here for the first time a form of grammatical construction, frequent in the Qur'an, that challenges the reader's sagacity. Phrases that are extremely concise constantly use pronouns and it is not always clear to whom or to what the pronoun refers. Hence the hesitation of the reader (and even the professional commentator) who is uncertain which sense to choose. The role of pronouns in the style of the Qur'an merits careful examination. It is rare for a phrase to have both its subject and its object or objects all represented by complete nouns. Usually one or the other of these nouns is expressed in a preceding statement, and in the phrase that concerns us, a pronoun appears in its place. Hence the lightness and incisive character of the style.

Sometimes the sense of the pronoun is clear; at other times the reader is puzzled.

Take, for example, these lines from the preceding text: 'This is naught but a revelation revealed, one terrible in power taught it him.'

Revelation thus appears as 'it' in the second verse. But the Arabic pronoun rendered here by 'it', which is masculine in Arabic, could equally apply to Muhammad, and one would then have 'taught him'. By translating 'it him', we decline the choice and give the two possibilities.

The reader's perplexity in the face of this uncertainty produces a feeling similar to that deliberately engendered by 'modern' novels in the West today, a kind of disorientation, a flight beyond time and place. The feeling is further intensified by phrases that refuse to define the content in order to give the impression that it is inexpressible:

'He revealed to His servant what He revealed.'

'When there covered the Lote-tree that which covered it.'

This characteristic feature of the style helps to emphasize a variety of meanings. Here, where the subject is God and His message, it expresses at the same time the profound, mysterious nature of revelation, the content of which cannot be circumscribed. It is what it is. Thus God defined Himself to Moses in the Book of Exodus.

In addition, this manner of speaking also means: it is not your concern. This last idea is often found in the Qur'an. Power consists in doing what one wants, without having to account to anyone else. That is the way God acts: He does what He wants. Here the listener is invited to worship and not to persist: He revealed what He revealed.

The Lote-tree of the Boundary and the Garden, designated by the word 'abode', may once have been familiar to listeners. Today it is impossible to say exactly what these words refer to. They have been the source of numerous interpretations by Muslim commentators, especially by the mystics. Is it a locale in paradise, at the boundary of heaven, or quite prosaically a place name near Mecca?

But the most important thing is to determine clearly who the person is that is referred to in the passage. It can only be Muhammad, as Muslim tradition has always maintained. The person the text calls 'your companion' is necessarily a contemporary, as the word is never applied to people in the past. The text proclaims the authenticity of his inspiration and dismisses any idea of mental aberration or transports of emotion.

To put the whole thing in its context, it is useful to recall some of the objections that the Meccans of the time levelled against Muhammad, objections that the Qur'an itself reports. They called him a soothsayer and a poet, and said he was possessed by jinn, thus suggesting that his inspiration verged on sorcery and arose from a dubious, demonic source. They accused him of merely repeating old stories that others had taught him.

In the present passage, as in Qur'an 81. 22–29, the text responds with an appeal to the visions, but there is very little information about them; everything is attributed to a superhuman being that Muhammad saw. This passage must be completed by the many traditions that have sought to explain it.

The man who opposes the preaching of Islam

'Nay, verily, man is insolent, for he thinks himself self-sufficient. Verily, to thy Lord is the return. Hast thou seen him who forbids a servant when he prays? Hast thou seen if he follows the true guidance or enjoins piety? Hast thou seen if he denies the truth, and turns away? Does he not know that God sees? Nay, verily, if he desist not, We shall seize him by the forelock, a lying, sinful forelock. So let him call on his council! We shall call on the guards of Hell. Nay, obey him not, but prostrate thyself, and draw near' (Qur'an 96. 6–29).

This text and the one that follows have been chosen to show two types of opposition that Muhammad had to face from the beginning of his ministry. The descriptions are vivid. They do not set out to present a picture of reality with all its nuances, but to pass judgment and to drive the listener to adhere to it.We are faced with a re-reading of certain historical facts about the early days of Islam. Is the subject man in general or a specific man, as the commentators say? It is impossible to know. He opposes Muhammad's message: he will be condemned. God sees him; to Him he will return. Hell awaits him with the Archangels who watch over the fire. On that day no tribal solidarity will serve to protect or save him.

The passage betrays profound emotion. The style is breathless and interrupted by questions and appeals. Three times an exclamation, found in other suras of the same period, re-echoes like a cry of protest at this vile conduct: Nay, verily! Blachère's translation renders it as 'Take care', with an overtone of menace. Other translations merely say 'Nay' or else repeat 'Nay, nay.'

The opponent is a rich man. The Qur'an often returns to the fact that wealth is both a blessing and a trial that can deflect from Islam. There is pride in wealth and power: man can be carried away when he thinks he can do without others. This is the case with the rebel who protests against law and authority or sets himself up as a tyrant.

The rebuke extends beyond a particular man to the rich Meccans who rejected Muhammad's message until he emerged as manifestly the more powerful. Does this mean that the first Muslims were poor men, as some have maintained? Such a claim would not be correct.

There was a social problem in Mecca. Commercial life,

centred on the city, had introduced the rule of money. The tribal solidarity of the desert, which had ensured that the poor were cared for by the community, had been greatly weakened. Therefore Islam, with its bonds of brotherhood, appeared from some points of view to represent social reform. The first Muslims brought together faithful who came from all classes of society. There were young men and men who were not so young, but all less than forty years old, and some of them belonged to families who had been powerful one or two generations ago. Khadija and Abu Bakr were rich. Former slaves like the freedman Bilal had almost nothing.

In this text, the wicked rich man forbids the poor man to pray. This is an allusion to the sometimes savage harassment suffered by the first converts. The wicked rich man calls Muhammad's preaching (which is implied) a lie. The threat follows at once: God sees him, Hell awaits him. And the whole passage ends with a warning: do not obey him, prostrate yourself and draw near to God.

A curse addressed to Muhammad's own uncle, Abu Lahab

'In the name of God the Merciful, the Compassionate

Perish the hands of Abu Lahab, and perish he! His wealth and his gains shall avail him not. He shall be burnt in a flaming fire, and his wife, the carrier of the firewood, with a rope of palm-fibre upon her neck' (Qur'an, Sura 111, passim).

The last text that rounds off this series devoted to pre-Islamic Mecca and the early days of Muslim preaching completes the picture of the opposition. It concerns a curse, addressed to Muhammad's own uncle who had always refused to listen to his nephew. The theme is simple: he will perish, he has perished . . . His power (a word that in the Arabia of that time meant sons, livestock and possessions) has not protected him. He will burn in hellfire. His wife, who had placed a bundle of thorns, fastened by a piece of rope, in Muhammad's path at night to trip him, will meet a punishment to fit her sin in hell.

The text is harsh. It is important to be aware of it, for it throws a useful light on one of the aspects of Islam. The Muslim, with his eyes riveted on Muhammad, sees the persecution suffered by the prophet when he called people to Islam and fulfilled his commission. In his presence men are divided into friends and enemies, good and bad. Enemies must be rendered powerless. Friends, on the other hand, will be treated as such.

It is difficult to date the text precisely. Does it come from the time when Muhammad began to preach to his people, as Qur'an 26. 215–220 ordered him to do? Or, on the other hand, does it date from his uncle's death around 624? At all events, it is quite consistent with the image of the Muslim given in Sura 48, verse 29: 'Hard against the unbelievers, merciful to one another.' We have here a very human policy in the struggle for power. In his *Little Red Book*, fourteen centuries after the Qur'an, Mao Tse-Tung gave a similar directive: 'Our army has always favoured a twofold policy: on the one hand, we are implacable to the enemy . . . , on the other, we are good to our own . . . and we must look to our unity' (beginning of Chapter 13).

The question is, however, more complex. If harshness is presented by the Qur'an as the necessary response of violence to violence, it is nonetheless tempered at other times, when clemency is possible or preferable. We see this harshness in Abraham, who, in the latest suras of the Qur'an, refuses to pray for his father when there is no longer hope for the latter's conversion (Qur'an 9. 114), and in Noah, whom God orders not to have pity on the fate of his unbelieving son (Qur'an 11. 45–57). In the same way, Abraham receives the command not to intercede for Sodom and Gomorrah (Qur'an 11. 74–76). A warrior people must not be swayed by compassion at a time when victory depends on their firmness. Later on they can think again.

There is another picture of the opponent who is punished in Qur'an 74. 11–56. In the end, the account encompasses the Last Judgment and gives a list of the offences that lead to damnation: refusing to join those who say the ritual prayer, neglecting to feed the poor, arguing and rejecting Muhammad's message by calling it a lie.

This survey has introduced the reader to an initial choice of texts. We must now go on to examine other themes. For it is characteristic of the didactic method of the Qur'an that, although it appeals to a small number of principles that are constantly repeated, it brings them into play almost simultaneously when it is useful to do so to gain assent. There are no distinctions made according to the period or literary form as in the Bible. In the Qur'an, Adam is a perfect Muslim, after his repentance, and he knows as much about the faith as Jesus does.

Our task, therefore, is to become familiar as soon as possible with the main lines of the teaching: the sense of the majesty of God the Creator, the place of man in the world, the sacred books and the prophets, the Last Things, the mission of the community in the world, and so on. This will be the aim of the following chapters.

3

Hymns to God the Creator

Creation, in the Qur'an, has a place of paramount importance. First of all, because it is often repeated that God is the Creator of heaven and earth, and that all things come from Him; but also because creation appears as the most characteristic manifestation of His power and His goodness. God created mankind and jinn to worship Him (Qur'an 51. 56). He created other living things as well for the sustenance of man and also as a final reward for the just who have surmounted the trials of life.

The Qur'an often argues from the self-evident facts of creation. It does not stop to prove the existence of God; for men of that time, His existence was not in question. On the other hand, it is concerned to demonstrate that God is one.

Meditation on creation

It is by meditating on creation that the Qur'an invites man to rise towards God. The Qur'an even exhorts man to devote himself unremittingly to this practice:

'Surely in the creation of the heavens and the earth and in the alternation of night and day, there are signs for men of understanding who remember God, standing and sitting and reclining, and reflect upon the creation of the heavens and the earth: "Our Lord, Thou hast not created this in vain. Glory be to Thee! Preserve us from the torment of the Fire'" (Qur'an 3. 190–191).

Creation in the Qur'an is in line with biblical tradition

In the Qur'an, there is no coherent account of creation, as in the first two chapters of the book of Genesis, and yet the tradition is the same. God created the world in six days (for example, Qur'an 50.38). The first man to be created was Adam. But true to its usual practice, the Qur'an confines itself to generalities, putting all the emphasis on the lesson to be learned. Unlike Genesis, it gives none of the naive details criticized by those who have no appreciation of poetic expression and who continually demand the most limited kind of accuracy. Furthermore, the actual literary genre of the Qur'an puts it beyond the criticisms that have been levelled at the Bible. At some points it allows its own tendency to break through, as in the frequent affirmation of the transcendence of God. It rejects the image of God resting on the seventh day. In the same way it is no longer Adam who gives things their names; it is God who teaches Adam what they are. Thus a power is attributed directly to God that Genesis recognizes to have been delegated to man.

Some unusual details, however, show that the Qur'an, following Genesis, reflects the expectations and knowledge of the age. It mentions seven heavens, celestial spheres and the sun floating towards its resting place (cf. Qur'an 67. 3; 36. 38–40), as well as shooting stars whose function is to stone over-curious demons (Qur'an 67. 5; 72. 8–9). This mode of expression serves to convey the religious lesson.

The usefulness of the divine gifts and man's gratitude

To oblige man to show his gratitude, the Qur'an multiplies the reminders of what God has given him. The evidence lies in the repetition of the expression 'for you' in some passages. God did this for you. He created that for you . . .

Descriptions of nature often provide lists of beings, pointing to a characteristic feature of each of them. These descriptions are sober and restrained and their powerful impact stems from this restraint and the truth of the scenes that are portrayed.

In the Qur'an there is none of the exuberant imagination found in Psalm 104 with the description of the water that surges through the mountains and all that happens to it along the way, nor even the simple, beautiful reflection on creation which appears in the book of Genesis: 'And God saw that it was good.' This is due to two different attitudes towards the same mystery. The psalm sings of the grandeur and splendour of creation, signs of the grandeur and splendour of God, but it is up to man himself to extract the lesson. The Qur'an, on the other hand, makes sure that man does not remain at the level of the created order but that he turns at once to God. It guides his reflection.

Plants and animals which appear in the Qur'an

The restraint of the style means that comparatively few creatures are referred to in the Qur'an. If one wanted to found a zoo or a botanical garden with the plants and animals mentioned in the different suras, one would not end up with a very large park. It would be a bestiary that reflected daily life in Arabia, plus some species that the pagan Arabs considered to be sacred or forbidden, with the addition of some animals that are famous in history like Jonah's fish (Qur'an 37. 142), the wolf that did not eat Joseph (Qur'an 12. 16), the red heifer of the Pentateuch (Qur'an 2. 67, cf. in the Bible Numbers 19), the camel that had to pass through the needle's eye (Qur'an 7. 40), an apocalyptic beast (Qur'an 27. 82) . . . And, among the tiny insects, the bee and its hives, the fly that the false gods do not create, and the collection of animals that appear in the plagues of Egypt (locusts, lice, frogs; Qur'an 7. 133), ending with the mosquito that God does not hesitate to cite in His parables (Qur'an 2. 24).

There is a similar restraint in the case of plants. Crops (a word that seems to mean cereals), olive trees, palm trees, vines and pomegranates constitute the background. A few desert trees complete the picture with, lastly, some images familiar from the earlier religious tradition, such as the seven ears of corn in Joseph's dream (Qur'an 12. 43–47), or even, with some amplification, the grain that bears fruit and gives seven ears of a hundred grains each, whereas the sower in the Gospel gets at best a hundred for one (Qur'an 2. 261), and so on.

Some passages in the Qur'an are hymns to the Creator

There are a number of suras (especially Meccan) in which allusions to nature play an important part. As they glance through the Qur'an, readers will slowly come to know them.

By way of example, we will consider one of the passages that are dedicated to God the Creator and are real hymns. It is a good idea, when we come across such excerpts, to read and re-read them several times, to see how the text is structured, with words that recur frequently and stereotyped expressions that are repeated, sometimes in a slightly modified form, from one line to another. Above all it is a good idea to note the attributes of God to which appeal is made: compassion, wisdom, power, and so on. A study of this kind will enable us to elicit the lesson more easily in each case.

Here, then, is the hymn that we are going to read carefully. There are others which will be pointed out later. Readers should tackle these on their own; if they do, they will discover a great many verses that evoke different aspects of creation scattered throughout the text. The 'He' at the beginning of the following hymn refers to God.

Hymn to the Creator in Qur'an 16. 3–18

3   He created the heavens and the earth in truth; high be He exalted above all that they associate with Him!

4   He created man from a sperm-drop; and, behold, he is an open disputer.

5   And the cattle – He created them for you; in them is warmth and uses various, and of them you eat;

6   And there is beauty in them for you, when you bring them home and when you drive them forth to pasture;

7   And they bear your loads to lands that you could not reach, save with great trouble. Surely your Lord is kind and merciful.

8   And horses, and mules, and asses, for you to ride, and as an adornment; and He creates what you know not.

9   It is for God to show the way; and some do swerve from it. If He had willed, He would have guided you all aright.

10   It is He who sends down to you water from the sky: from which you have drink, and from it are trees, for you to pasture your herds.

11   And thereby He brings forth for you crops, and olives, and palms, and vines, and all manner of fruit. Surely in this is a sign for a people who reflect.

12   And He subjected to you the night and the day, and the sun and the moon; and the stars are subjected by His command. Surely in this are signs for a people who understand.

13 And that which He has created for you in the earth of diverse hues. Surely in this is a sign for a people who remember.

14 It is He who subjected to you the sea, that you may eat of it fresh flesh, and take forth from it ornaments for you to wear; and thou seest the ships ploughing through it; and that you may seek His bounty, and so haply you will be thankful.

15 And He cast on the earth firm mountains, lest it shake with you, and rivers and paths; so haply you will be guided.

16 And landmarks; and by the stars they are guided.

17 Is then He who creates as he who does not create? Will you not remember?

18 If you would count God's blessings, you could never number them. Surely God is forgiving, compassionate.

An initial reading shows that, in this passage, God is first and foremost the Creator: not only did He create, but His creative action is continually exerted as He makes the crops grow, subdues the sea, and so on. All the activities of nature are attributed to Him. This mode of discourse that extols the sole First Cause is commonplace in the religious texts of Islam, Christianity and Judaism. There is nothing surprising here and other passages develop the theme.

The divine attributes that are emphasized above are goodness, mercy and forgiveness (verses 7 and 18). Hence the duty of gratitude (verse 14), and the first and principal feature of this gratitude is to proclaim the oneness of God, since no other god participated in creation (verse 17).

The whole hymn is like a series of pictures. The subject is everyday life, the animals familiar in Arabia, the resources of the Red Sea, the nomads' migrations, the vegetation of the oases, the framework of day and night ... The text recalls important benefits enjoyed by man but it does not seek to list them all. Other passages in the Qur'an amplify it. There is no mention here of the creation of woman to which allusion is made elsewhere (Qur'an 30. 21). And the creation of man at the beginning of the hymn is there only to contrast his insignificance with his pretentions as a disputer, and thus to extol once again the omnipotence of God. The mysterious aspect of creation appears clearly only once (verse 8), when it is said that God creates 'what you know not'. Elsewhere this thought underlies all the enumerations.

Thus creation is put at the centre of Muslim religious thought and, in everyday life, one continually meets believers who praise God as the author of all benefits. The great sin condemned by the mystics consisted in giving so much weight to secondary causes that one forgot the supreme Reality, the One who exists by Himself and who is the origin of all created beings, God.

The beauty and excellence of creation is described: sufficiently for the listener to grasp its worth but without lingering too long to savour it. The text is there to attribute everything to God. The rhythm is distinctive and probably adapted to Muslim susceptibilities, offering sententious sayings intended to be imprinted on the memory and repeated as ejaculatory prayers.

This is poles apart from a naturalism that exalts nature for its own sake. If the believer is tempted to stop along the way and delight in created things as an end in themselves, the text sees to it that he is called to order, badgering him and giving him no respite. This badgering is perhaps one of the features that most strikes non-Muslim readers, the first time they come across such passages.

The lines are certainly very vivid. They are most effective when recited in a setting of similar scenes of rural and nomadic life.

The Qur'an's didacticism appears here in all its amplitude. There is a sense of the obvious throughout the whole extract: once the spiritual attitude of the Muslim has been adopted, there is no further place for anxiety. Suffering and sin scarcely appear; there is merely a reference to the sin of rebelliousness ('man is an open disputer'), that is, ingratitude or polytheism, and at the end the word of forgiveness returns us to the same plane of reality. Here the Qur'an demands of the reader the only basic attitude appropriate for the creature in the presence of his all-powerful Creator.

The structure of the hymn

From the point of view of composition, this hymn to creation is clearly structured, with a carefully contrived, gradual development that leads to the high point of the last verse: 'If you would count God's blessings, you could never number them.'

The hymn can be divided into several groups of verses, always remembering that this kind of division is necessarily arbitrary.

First, there is a general allusion to the creation of the heavens and earth and man, followed at once by two practical reactions: a proclamation of monotheism and a rebuke to man for his opposition (understood as being to the message brought by Muhammad). In Arabic, each of the two verses is relatively short, with two parts that are well balanced. The tonality of the letters, the rhythm of the syllables and the music of the sounds in Arabic also play a part in the impression that is conveyed (verses 3 and 4).

A second group describes cattle and ends with the thought of what God does without man's knowledge. In the middle of this group, the reference to God who is kind and merciful is the first expression of a previously diffuse idea that will be asserted more and more clearly until it finally dominates the conclusion of the extract. A hymn to the Creator, this passage is a call for gratitude.

Verse 9 expresses an idea that, at first sight, would appear to be slightly different. In fact, it serves as a preacher's digression. It concerns a road and a journey: man's great, long journey is the one that leads him towards God, and the text merely reminds him of the fact. The Qur'an takes advantage of every opportunity to exhort, instruct and impress its doctrine on the mind and emotional consciousness of the believer.

Also to be noted is the use of the pronoun 'you' (for *you*, *your* loads) and the second person plural of the verbs. This is a summons to man, the farmer and caravaneer... Thus it stresses the utility of animals and the prestige they bring. It is a good idea to read and re-read these five verses in order fully to grasp the structure (verses 5 to 9).

A third group is devoted to fresh water and vegetation; but here the insistence on the lesson to be drawn becomes more urgent. Three verses conclude with a reference to the signs represented by these phenomena or gifts: 'Surely in this is a sign for . . .', etc. We find here one of the Qur'an's literary devices that surprises the reader with expressions that he does not expect. Sometimes we have one sign, sometimes signs in the plural. It is the same with reflection, understanding and the act of remembering. And with the reference to a sign the horizon expands: to water and vegetation are added the sky and stars and, in contrast to night or the fruits of daylight, different hues, a sober description of the dazzling display of colours that shine out over the whole world (verses 10 to 13).

The words reflection and understanding create an atmosphere. In fact the aim is to induce admiration and gratitude. This last element is introduced imperceptibly, like the first appearance of a theme in a symphony: after this appeal, the believer instinctively waits to see what will follow. There have been earlier descriptions of the sea, travels, mountains, rivers and the whole environment that affects a people of caravaneers and travellers like the Arabs. This point is stressed by some commentators.

The usefulness of created things is again made explicit. God's blessings often refer to the benefits of trade, in the Qur'anic style, and that is the case here. In short, when the time comes that gratitude is demanded of the believer, the text has prepared the ground so well that he cannot refuse (verses 14 to 26).

Finally, in the midst of terms referring to travel that return to an idea raised at the beginning of the hymn (with the role of cattle in transport), the rhythm of the enumerations is about to be broken. Suddenly, as if enough was now known about nature, or perhaps as if to say that the most important thing lies elsewhere, the listener is pulled up short by a question; all that has gone before now appears to have been simply a cogent preparation for a solemn declaration: 'Is He who creates as he who does not create?'

The break in the very course of the exposition signifies that it is useless to continue to enumerate the wonders of creation. The person who does not understand the first time that God is one, will not grasp it any better if the examples are multiplied: it will serve no purpose (verse 17).

In the end the passage quietens down with the affirmation of the infinite goodness of God. And as is often the case in the Qur'an, it is the final word that places us ever more clearly in God's presence. It is no longer a matter of creatures and benefits but of God alone and His attributes: 'Surely God is forgiving, compassionate' (verse 18).

This stylistic device is a way of conveying the sense of the divine names by presenting them in the light of all that has been said. Divine mercy manifests itself in nature and its gifts for us. The presence of forgiveness may seem surprising, since there has been little mention of sin in the preceding verses. Is it a reference to opposition? To polytheism? Or is it perhaps also a way of reminding us that the polytheists, too, benefit from all these material gifts of nature: if God bestows the latter on them it is out of pure kindness . . . ? Elsewhere in the Qur'an forgiveness appears in connection with paradise. Since in Islam sin is not a breach in the life with God, it does not have the same resonance as in Christianity. It is an evil act for which God has the right to punish the author and if God, in spite of everything, grants the material benefits of nature to the guilty, it is by virtue of forgiveness. In some respects, forgiveness is equivalent to permission to enjoy the good things that punishment could have withheld from the guilty. The commentary of Jalalain explains the term compassionate as follows: 'In so far as He grants you favours despite your inadequacies and your disobedience.'

Brief references to other hymns to the Creator

The following references indicate texts that readers can tackle by themselves. Their first task should be to look for the divine attributes that the passage seeks to emphasize.

For example: the power and wisdom of God at the end of a long text on divine blessings (Qur'an 30. 17–27). To be noted, too, is the place of the idea of the sign. The excerpt also contains a verse on the creation of the spouses God has given to men (verse 21) together with the affection that ensues. It could be compared to the creation of Eve in Genesis.

Another passage (Qur'an 27. 59–64) has as a refrain the question: 'Is there a god with God?'

One extract shows how God interrogates man in the Qur'an. It is not man who interrogates God: the Qur'an has no passages like the complaints of Job in the Bible. Here God speaks to man as He does at the end of the Book of Job. It would be interesting to compare the gist of the questions in the two cases to see which elements each one emphasizes. Here man is compelled to acknowledge that he is of no significance, that everything has been created by God and given to him. Moreover, had God so wished, these benefits could have disappeared (Qur'an 56. 57–74).

Finally, attention must be drawn to a stylistic device that is sometimes employed to demonstrate the contingency of beings: they are all in the hands of God. The Qur'an either makes an assumption (If God had wished, this or that would have been otherwise – cf. Qur'an 56. 70), or else it interrogates man (Are you sure that . . . for example, the earth will not swallow you up in a cataclysm? – cf. Qur'an 67. 16, 17, 30).

The passages on creation in the Qur'an are too numerous for it to be possible to cite them all. To those already indicated, we need add only the most important: Qur'an 6. 95–99; 13. 2, 8–15, 17; 16. 65–70; 35. 11–14, 27–28; 36. 33–44, 68–73; 55. 1–34.

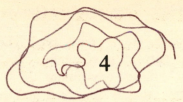

4

Adam, Father of Humankind

Every religion and every philosophy has its own distinctive conception of man, even if it does not proclaim it at once. This conception sometimes appears in statements of principle, but more often emerges in an actual way of life.

The Qur'an does not dwell on long theoretical considerations, but the kind of existence it describes implies a whole anthropology. In relation to God the Creator and Lord of the universe, man is first and foremost a creature from whom God demands worship (Qur'an 51. 56). Above all he must recognize that God is his Lord and Master (Qur'an 7. 172); he must surrender to Him and regard none as His equal.

The biological aspect of human life is mentioned so that man may know his place, recognize that he is small and weak and not become proud. Before he is born, it is not even known which sex he will be; he experiences long periods of weakness before becoming strong and then he returns to weakness. Later he departs this life. These obvious truths that are set before the faithful are often expressed in a striking way:

'No soul knows in what land it shall die' (Qur'an 31. 43).

The distinctively human aspect of life, characterized by work, thought and choices, appears at every turn. The reader is introduced to a patriarchal world with its respect for father and mother, pastoral and agricultural activity and even the exploitation of the sea (fishing, coral, pearls, etc.). The reference to travel presupposes a network of communication, trade and the whole art of ship-building and navigation.

The Qur'an takes men as they are and commends the natural, social values that are found in all societies governed by the Decalogue. It reminds them that they are not alone in the world, free to act according to their whim or caprice. The pagans resented Islam, which put a curb on the right to property, associating it with duties. For God leaves man free on condition that he respects certain laws. The Qur'an appeals to the intellect, reflection and memory. It promises man happiness in this world and the next. But in case of conflict between the two, the concerns of the hereafter take precedence.

It does seem that Islam is a man's religion that glorifies force in the service of justice, the solidarity of the group, generosity and the protection of its weak members, and sees woman primarily as a mother. It advocates self-control as in Ramadan but, at the same time, this effort is only temporarily imposed and is then followed by relaxation.

Islam appears to be an easy religion: it refuses to accept that man should abstain from the good things that God has created for him. Muslim marriage does not entail the same demands as Christian marriage. Moreover in life, righteous hatred and violence are sometimes tolerated or even encouraged. Islam is categorically opposed to the idea of original sin, although it knows that man is a prey to the temptations of Satan and his own sensuality. At bottom, man is insignificant: he is not fundamentally a sinner.

Heroism has a place especially in the struggle for ideals. At times the believer may be called upon to give his life for the faith. This is not necessarily in the case of persecution, for he then has the right to dissimulate if he cannot avoid death in any other way (Qur'an 16. 106), but it is called for in the case of holy war. Faith is compared to a commercial contract: God purchases the Muslim's life and promises him paradise in exchange (Qur'an 61. 10–12).

The glorification of the greatness of God could make it seem that, as an indirect consequence, man is overshadowed: this is not so at all. For, in another light, man is the vicegerent of God on earth and, in so far as he is a Muslim, shares in the authority and power of the God he serves, with whom he has a special relationship and whose rule he strives to extend on earth.

The situation of man in relation to God appears most notably in the account of the origins of humanity. In fact the Qur'an contains several recensions of the story of the creation of Adam and his fall and expulsion from the earthly paradise. We propose to examine them now.

A study of the three passages that are reproduced here introduces the reader to a new domain, that of Qur'anic texts from different periods which treat the same subject in parallel. Thus in the Qur'an there are several accounts of Noah and the Flood, the destruction of the city of Lot, the relations between Moses and Pharaoh, and so on. And in this particular place we have three versions of the fall of the angels and Adam from the earthly paradise, to say nothing of other texts treating specific passages from this series which we shall not be examining.

Adam, Iblis, Their Creation and Their Tests

The oldest text (Qur'an 20. 115–124)	Text proclaimed shortly before the Hijra (Qur'an 7. 11–24)	The latest text (at Medina, after 622) (Qur'an 2. 30–39)
115 And of old We made a covenant with Adam, but he forgot, and We found in him no constancy.		30 And when thy Lord said to the angels, 'I am about to place a viceroy in the earth,' they said, 'What, wilt Thou place in it one who will spread corruption, and shed blood, while we proclaim Thy praise and hallow Thy name?' He said, 'Verily, I know what you know not.' (There follows the episode in which God teaches Adam the names of things . . .)
116 And when We said to the angels, 'Prostrate yourselves before Adam,' they prostrated themselves, save Iblis; he refused.	11 We created you, then We formed you, then We said to the Angels, 'Prostrate yourselves before Adam;' so they prostrated themselves, save Iblis – he was not among those who prostrated themselves.	34 And when We said to the angels, 'Prostrate yourselves before Adam,' they prostrated themselves, save Iblis; he refused in his pride, and so he became one of the unbelievers.

12 Said He, 'What pre-
vented thee from
prostrating thyself,
when I commanded
thee?' Said he, 'I
am better than he;
Thou hast created
me of fire, but him
Thou hast created
of clay.'

13 Said He, 'Get thee
down hence; it is not
for thee to show
pride here, so go
thou forth; surely
thou art among the
humbled.'

14 Said he, 'Respite me
till the day they shall
be raised.'

15 Said He, 'Thou art
among the ones that
are respited.'

16 Said he, 'Now, be-
cause Thou hast
caused me to err, I
shall surely lie in
wait for them on
Thy straight path;

17 Then I shall come
upon them from
before and from
behind, from their
right hand and from
their left; Thou wilt
not find most of
them thankful.'

18 Said He, 'Go forth from it, despised and banished. If any of them follow thee – I shall assuredly fill hell with all of you.'

117 Then We said, 'O Adam, surely this is an enemy to thee and thy wife. So let him not drive you both out of the Garden, so that thou art miserable.

19 'O Adam, dwell thou and thy wife in the Garden, and eat of where you will, but come not nigh this tree, lest you become wrong-doers.'

35 And We said, 'O Adam! dwell thou and thy wife in the Garden, and eat freely thereof wherever you desire; but draw not nigh this tree, lest you become wrong-doers.'

118 For to thee it is given neither to hunger therein, nor to go naked,

119 Neither to suffer from thirst, nor from the heat of the sun.'

120 Then Satan whispered to him saying, 'O Adam, shall I point thee to the Tree of Immortality, and a kingdom that decays not?'

20 Then Satan whispered to them, to reveal to them their nakedness, which had been hidden from them. He said, 'Your Lord has only forbidden you this tree lest you become angels, or lest you become immortals.'

36 Then Satan caused them to slip there-from and brought them out of the state in which they were.

21 And he swore to them, 'Truly, I am for you a sincere adviser.'

121 So the two of them ate of it, and their nakedness appeared to them, and they began to sew upon themselves leaves of the Garden. And Adam disobeyed his Lord, and so went astray.

22 So he led them on by deceit; and when they tasted the tree, their nakedness appeared to them, and they began to sew upon themselves leaves of the Garden. And their Lord called to them, 'Did I not forbid you this tree, and say to you, "Verily Satan is for you a manifest foe?"'

122 Thereafter his Lord chose him, and relented towards him, and guided him.

23 They said, 'O our Lord, we have wronged ourselves, and if Thou dost not forgive us, and have mercy upon us, we shall surely be among the lost.'

123 Said He, 'Get you down hence, both of you together, enemies one to the other; but if there comes to you from Me guidance, then whosoever follows My guidance shall not go astray, neither shall he be miserable.

24 Said He, 'Get you down, in enmity one to the other. On earth a dwelling-place shall be yours, and enjoyment for a time.' Said He, 'There you shall live, and there you shall die, and from there you shall be brought forth.'

36 We said, 'Get you down, enemies one to another; and in the earth a dwelling-place shall be yours, and enjoyment for a time.'

37 Then Adam received words from his Lord, and He turned towards him; for He is the Relenting, the Merciful.

124 But whosoever turns away from the remembrance of Me, his shall be a life of narrowness, and We shall raise him up blind on the Day of Resurrection.'

38 We said, 'Get you down from here, all together; yet there shall come to you guidance from Me, and whosoever follows My guidance, no fear shall be on them, nor shall they grieve.

39 But those who disbelieve and deny Our signs, they shall be Companions of the Fire; in it shall they remain for ever.'

The angels' test

The first subject is the angels and their fall. They are already in existence at the beginning of the narrative when God announces that He is going to create Adam. The prospect does not seem to please them and they voice their objections. This is a way of calling attention to man's faults, his depravity and the bloody conflicts of which he will be guilty.

God then orders the angels to prostrate themselves before Adam. This scene has always intrigued historians of Judaism and Christianity. It is otherwise little known. A writer like Speyer, who has made an exhaustive study of the Jewish and Rabbinic texts containing narratives analogous to those in the Qur'an, comes to no clear conclusion. He assumes that the scene is connected with a Christian reinterpretation of Jewish traditions about the angels' rebellion that writers relate to the union between angels and the daughters of men (cf. Genesis 6.1: Speyer, *Die biblischen Erzählungen im Qoran*, Hildesheim 1961, 56ff.). This reinterpretation is found in *The Life of Adam and Eve*. Speyer stresses in this connection that the name Iblis is a simplification of *diabolos*: does this perhaps suggest a Christian context?

The Old and New Testaments contain only one allusion to the angelic origin of demons and that is in the Epistle of Jude, concerning angels 'who kept not their first estate but left their own habitation' (v. 9).

Iblis' pride and his noble origin (he was created from fire and not clay) are given as the motives for his refusal to pay homage to Adam. The text in Sura 7, which is quite similar to another parallel narrative (Qur'an 15. 26–42), finally grants Iblis his status as the enemy of man. He secures a respite from God: he will not be punished at once, although he is expelled from paradise (some exegetes say from heaven). God allows him to pit himself against men for a time.

Iblis' attitude is presented as a kind of revenge on God. Iblis works off his own frustration. He tempts man because he himself is damned: all his rancour bursts out in the pronoun 'Thy'. 'I shall surely lie in wait for them on Thy straight path', he says to God, referring to the path on which, in prayer, the Muslim asks to be rightly guided. And Iblis waylays men, trips them up and leads them astray. The rest of the narrative sets the temptation, Iblis-Satan's work, at the centre of the story of Adam and his wife.

Why is there this prolonged insistence on the angel's sin, whereas Adam's is dealt with more cursorily? Why especially is Iblis so articulate: speaking, provoking and attacking in a free and easy way, while Adam opens his mouth only once and then, in unison with his wife, to acknowledge his fault unhesitatingly? Why do the texts as a whole give Iblis a certain personality while Adam has hardly any? Iblis will not escape from God but he has a respite and, in the meantime, he profits from it: he diverts man from the straight path and prevents him from being grateful to God when gratitude is an essential duty for a Muslim. He is truly the Enemy in the full sense of the word, and this is the reason why such importance is given to him.

Adam and his wife

The scene in the earthly paradise is less detailed in the Qur'an than in Genesis. In the Qur'an, God places Adam and his wife in the garden without revealing her name. It is, in fact, the usual Qur'anic practice to designate women in terms of their relation to their husbands: for example, the wives of Abraham, Lot and Pharaoh. The name of Mary, mother of Jesus, is the only one that is mentioned explicitly.

In paradise, Adam and his wife could eat anything except from the forbidden tree. Genesis mentions two trees that they are not allowed to touch. In the Qur'an, there is only one and we are not told what kind of tree it is. Iblis alone provides details. He speaks of the tree of immortality (Qur'an 20. 120). But can Iblis' words be trusted? The style is extremely skilful. In fact, the reader will never be sure what happened. An air of ambiguity surrounds Iblis-Satan. This is perhaps to ensure that man knows that the most important thing does not lie here. The most important thing is the disobedience to God and the subsequent punishment.

The temptation itself is unilateral. Iblis alone speaks: moreover one of his remarks is curious and is cited by a commentator like Fakhr al-Din al-Razi. To tempt Adam and his wife, Iblis-Satan tells them that God has forbidden them to eat of this tree only to prevent them from becoming angels. But if angels have to prostrate themselves before Adam, why should Adam want to become one? The answer distinguishes between different categories of angel and confirms the attraction to Adam, despite everything, of the idea of belonging to the superior category of these beings. Adam and Eve themselves are passive. They eat of the forbidden tree, but actually it is not very clear what takes place: the footlights and spotlights are not turned on for them. It is others who speak to them or about them. They themselves say nothing except for a sentence uttered together to ask forgiveness (Qur'an 7. 23).

The conclusion to be drawn from the whole narrative is simple. Among men, there are good and bad. Adam is good; temptation took him by surprise and he fell, but he got up at once, trusting in divine forgiveness and mercy. He surrendered to God. His experience ends with God's promise to guide men. It is an opportunity for the reader to be introduced to the prophetic dimension and to discover the first implicit announcement of Muhammad in the Muslim history of the world. God's mercy which, in the hymn to the Creator, gives men the benefits of nature, will grant them a series of prophets to guide them, with Muhammad as the glorious culmination of the series.

What of the human condition? Little is said about it. In paradise, man did not have to suffer as the nomad does: from hunger, thirst, cold and the sweltering sun. By contrast, when he is driven out of paradise, he is miserable. What is his position then? The text has little to say: he will be subject to concupiscence, as shown in the episode of his shame and the clothes fashioned from leaves, an episode that is amply developed. He will have a temporary dwelling-place and enjoyment on earth, he will die and then be restored to life. The texts describe the human condition rather than explaining it. Man has good days and bad days. Paradise was a happy chance . . . it is no more. Human life is presented as a journey. Satan is there to tempt and seduce men. They can escape him and regain happiness on one condition, that they follow the prophets whom God will send to guide them.

'Whosoever follows My guidance, no fear shall be on them, nor shall they grieve.'

A window on the future

This is the first instance of forgiveness in the history of humanity: God thus manifests a new form of mercy towards mankind. The reader will also have noted the reference to the Last Things. In Genesis, the parallel account enumerates the aspects of the human condition which, following Adam's sin, will weigh heavily on every man; it records that Satan's head will be crushed, but there is no word about the hereafter. The Qur'an, on the contrary, speaks here of life as it is, with its transient pleasures, demands and, above all, the end towards which it leads. Concupiscence, the hard struggle against Iblis-Satan and the hostility of men to each other are particularly stressed. But a two-fold hope appears. On the one hand, God promises to guide the faithful and, should they fall, offers His forgiveness; at the same time, He announces the eternal happiness of the just.

Other passages in the Qur'an also emphasize sin and forgiveness, which the text associates with certain characters: here it is Adam and the tree in paradise together with Iblis and his refusal; elsewhere it is the blatant splendour of Korah's wealth or Moses killing the Egyptian. These two examples are mentioned in connection with God's commands and the types of disobedience represented by different sins. Finally, the Last Judgment is the occasion for emphasizing the nature of the misdeeds that have led the guilty to disaster.

When it is regarded solely as a violation of God's commandments, and thus a violation of what has been forbidden, sin appears as absolute and shattering. Recently, a publication that appeared in Paris, seeking to compare Islam and Christianity, characterized Islam by its sense of sin. I wonder if this is true, or whether the sense of sin (and a Saviour who redeems from sin) is not, on the contrary, characteristic of true Christianity. It is, however, very clear that many (not all) Muslims live with the idea of what is forbidden and what is not constantly before them. Hence, some will use the expression 'it is a sin' to say that it is forbidden, it is not done, and a scrupulous conscience impels the sincere believer to avoid transgression.

Sin itself can be envisaged in different ways. Muslims obey and the best Muslims immediately add: we obey because it is a command and we love to obey God's commands. Conduct is not mere legalism but a desire to serve God; it is evidence of an openness of heart to God. This notion is linked to divine satisfaction. The Muslim longs for his conduct to please God, so that God may be satisfied with him. Thus we find in the Qur'an verses that say that God loves those who act in one way; He does not love those who act in another.

In Christianity and Islam, sin is seen in a different light, partly because the relation between God and man is not viewed from the same angle. In Islam, man is above all the servant of God, a servant who loves to serve his master. He is alone before Him and Islam emphatically rejects any mediator. Each man will bear his own burden: no one will carry the burden of another (cf. Qur'an 35. 18). Those who maintain the contrary are put in their place (Qur'an 29. 12–13). In the same way, no ransom will be accepted.

One expression sums up this position well. It stresses the fact that God is too exalted to be affected by human acts: man may harm himself by sinning; he does not harm God at all. The main Qur'anic word for sinner is 'wrongdoer', i.e. one who harms or does wrong. When a sinner repents and seeks forgiveness, he says: 'I have wronged myself.' Adam and Eve say this in the passage above (Qur'an 7. 23); the Queen of

Sheba uses the same words when she is converted to the worship of the one God in Solomon's presence. And there are also other characters in the Qur'an who speak in a similar vein.

The hereafter is barely described in the three texts that are presented, but as the faithful are very familiar with all the passages devoted to this theme in the Qur'an, a simple allusion suffices. The point to note is that the hereafter is announced to mankind from the beginning of humanity. According to Muslim dogma, Adam, Noah, Abraham, Moses and all the prophets believed in the resurrection of the dead and in heaven and hell. The resurrection is mentioned clearly in two of the preceding texts. It is assumed in the last one when it speaks of the Companions of the Fire, punished for eternity in contrast to the happiness of the just.

A last glance at the style

Muslims like to call attention to the many niceties of the style of the Qur'an: an example will illustrate this. It says in the Qur'an about Satan: 'So let him not drive you both out of the Garden, so that thou art miserable' (Qur'an 20. 117). The words in Arabic are short and resonant, but in particular the first verb is in the dual form, referring to Adam and Eve, while the second is in the masculine singular, referring to Adam alone. This creates a sense of surprise, for the masculine singular is unexpected. If there is a disaster, it is chiefly on Adam's shoulders that it will fall. We have here a telling depiction of the role of man in society.

Finally, notice the expression 'so that thou art miserable'. In narratives that deal with subjects in the past, the Qur'an sometimes has God foretell what is to come. For the listener who already knows or has heard the story, the new presentation, enhanced by predictions *post eventum*, attracts his attention, or better still his participation, as he remembers the rest, is proud of knowing it and is not likely to tire of hearing it. It is a way of saying once again that God knows everything in advance, that nothing happens unless He wills it.

5

Abraham, the Muslim

The history of humanity begins with Adam. According to Muslim teaching, the religion of mankind has always been the same. From the beginning, God revealed all that He wished to reveal and, in the sphere of doctrine, Adam knew as much as his descendants. The legislation alone has been modified by the successive Messengers of God. An axiom well known to Muslim theologians expresses this position. Throughout the ages there has been only one religion: 'Religion is one, laws are many.'

The essential element in religion is active, free and trusting submission to God, who is all-powerful and compassionate. This involves, on the one hand, recognizing His existence and His uniqueness and, on the other, putting oneself in His hands. This attitude of mind is rendered by the Arabic word *islām*, the Muslim being the one who puts himself in God's hands and obeys Him. Moreover, the Qur'an points out that this is the attitude of the whole of creation: creatures everywhere, whether they like it or not, obey, or in the end are obliged to obey, God:

Have they not seen all things that God has created casting their shadows to the right and to the left, prostrating themselves before God in all humility? To God bows everything in the heavens and on the earth, each thing that moves, and the angels. They are not proud' (Qur'an 16. 48–49).

Therefore man places himself in harmony with the whole

universe when he prostrates himself in prayer, his brow to the ground reflecting the shadows that also incline before God.

Since revelation is not progressive, Islam's religious ideals can be found in the conduct of all the men of God cited in the Qur'an. In the same way they were all Muslims: Adam, Idris (Enoch), Noah, Abraham, Isaac, Ishmael, Jacob, Joseph, Moses, Saul, David, Solomon, Elisha and so on, down to Zechariah, John the Baptist, Mary and Jesus.

I think that, for the Muslim, the man who received the grace to embody Islam most perfectly is Muhammad. But before him, in the Qur'an, the figure of Abraham has a special place. Going back in time beyond Jesus, whose Islam would be corrupted by Christians, and even beyond Moses, whose Islam would be corrupted by his followers, the Qur'an sees Abraham as the perfect Muslim and associates itself with him. Islam as preached by Muhammad is presented as a return to the pristine purity that it had in Abraham's time.

'Abraham was not a Jew, neither a Christian; but he was one pure of faith [a *ḥanīf*], a Muslim; and he was not of the idolaters. Surely the people who are nearest to Abraham are those who followed him, and this Prophet, and those who believe; and God is the Protector [Patron] of the believers' (Qur'an 3. 67–68).

This proclamation dates from the early years of the Muslim state in Medina, after the break with the Jews of the oasis. The Muslims who followed Muhammad (or, as the text says, 'those who followed this Prophet') are thus said to be the most authentic disciples of Abraham.

The text appeals to two ideas that appear elsewhere in the Qur'an. On the one hand, Abraham is called an independent monotheist [one pure of faith]. The term is a translation of an Arabic word [*ḥanīf*] that at that time referred to monotheists who refused to go over to Judaism or Christianity. On the other hand, God is called the 'patron' of believers. The word patron, or master, the term adopted by other translations, does not accurately translate the Arabic word, because of the distinctive nature of the forms of solidarity implied. In Islam, God is not called father. This term, which the Old Testament understands in a figurative sense, is systematically ruled out by Muslims. Some traditions are still prepared to compare God with a mother (as Isaiah already does), but a father is out of the question. The characteristic titles of God considered as ruler of the community of His creatures are Lord, in the strongest sense, of all creation (cf. Qur'an 7. 172), and *walī* in relation to believers. *Walī* is a word that suggests the strength of communal ties, either on the part of the leader of the community who is the *walī* in the sense of the patron or protector of his people, or on the part of the ordinary member who is a *walī*, in the sense of a friend of God. This word brings us back to the context of the 'people (or party) of God', the standard way in Islam of describing Muslims. God is a *walī* in so far as He is patron of his people.

Abraham surrendered himself to God, i.e. he was a Muslim, as is clearly taught in the Qur'anic quotation cited above. The most perfect example of this surrender is provided by the episode of the sacrifice of his son. The Qur'an has only one passage on the subject. The scene opens with the quotation of Abraham's prayer asking God for a son:

100   'My Lord, give me one of the righteous.'

101   Then We gave him the good tidings of a gentle son.

102   And when he had reached the age of walking with him, he said, 'O my son, I see in a dream that I shall sacrifice thee; consider, what is thy view?' He said: 'My father, do as thou art bidden; thou shalt find me, God willing, one of the steadfast.'

103   When they had both surrendered (to the will of God), and he laid him down upon his face,

104 We called unto him: 'O Abraham!

105 Thou hast fulfilled the vision.' Thus do We reward the righteous.

106 This was indeed a manifest trial.

107 And We ransomed him with a mighty sacrifice.

108 And We left this for him among the later folk:

109 'Peace be upon Abraham!' (Qur'an 37. 100–109).

This episode is a high point in the life of Abraham. He asks for a son: the mention of this wish, with all the yearning and hope that it implies, intensifies the deeply moving character of the renunciation that God will demand in return. Elsewhere, in the Qur'an, it is God Himself who announces the future birth. Abraham and his wife are advanced in years and, furthermore, the latter is barren. Several suras recall the visit of the guests, the calf killed in their honour, the promise of a son, and the departure of messengers who go to preside over the destruction of the city of Lot (Qur'an 51. 24–36; 11. 69–83).

'We gave her the glad tidings of Isaac, and, after Isaac, of Jacob' (Qur'an 11. 71).

Here, as in some other texts, Abraham is mentioned together with Isaac, Jacob and Lot without reference to Ishmael. But elsewhere, the descendants of Abraham are described as follows:

'Praise be to God, who has given me, in my old age, Ishmael and Isaac; surely my Lord is the Hearer of prayer' (Qur'an 14. 39).

To return to the text on the sacrifice, we find the main themes

of the narrative in Genesis repeated in a new version that has
its own distinction but does not put the emphasis in the same
place. Who is the son that Abraham takes to offer to God? The
text does not say and merely uses a general qualifier: he will be
gentle and calm, in keeping with character traits that are highly
prized by the Arabs. Many Muslim commentators, especially in
the early centuries, admitted that it was Isaac, but unanimous
opinion in the Muslim world increasingly inclines towards the
name of Ishmael.

In Genesis, the account has a tense, dramatic quality.
Scholars have often analysed the poignant sequence of words
attributed to God when He asks Abraham for his sacrifice.
'Take thy son, thine only son Isaac, whom thou lovest,
Isaac . . . ' (Genesis 22. 2). The crescendo emphasizes the
strength of the ties Abraham is called upon to break. Moreover, the thought of the promise is omnipresent: it is the only
beloved son, so long awaited, who risks being annihilated.
Later Abraham's silence as he makes his way with Isaac to the
place of sacrifice, and his evasive answers to the child's
questions, are profoundly tragic. The child, in Genesis, is
passive and wondering as he asks what is happening and shows
his disquiet in a respectful question.

In the Qur'an, everything is centred on the dialogue between
the father and son, as if the father was in need of comfort
before embarking on this dreadful adventure. The son is fully
informed and accepts the situation. The emotional focus is no
longer God's promise, which is called into question again in
Genesis, or Abraham's faith in the promise, but the quality of
his *islām*, which is shared by his son and the faith in his vision.
Both father and son obey.

Would it be too far-fetched to recall the theme of Jephthah's
daughter who also accepted death, only asking for a delay to go
with her friends to bewail her fate in the mountains? Or even,
more simply, does the generosity of some children make this
acceptance believable? In the Qur'an, which is addressed

primarily to men and to adults, the episode of this child makes a unique impression.

In the Qur'an, as in Genesis, the story is provided with a happy ending, with the reference to the ransom sacrifice which many Muslims (those who think that the son was Ishmael) place at Muna, near Mecca. From this perspective, the annual sacrifice at the pilgrimage becomes a reminder of Abraham's act when he offered an animal in place of the son who survived. And the sheep which are seen in the streets of every town in the Muslim world on the eve of the festival thus recall the ransom lamb.

After this sacrifice, in both the biblical and Qur'anic traditions, Abraham is called 'the friend of God', perhaps because he showed that his heart was innocent of all human ties.

Does the Qur'an provide geographical or historical information that would enable us to place Abraham in his milieu and age? Actually, it is quite pointless to look for facts of this kind. Like many other Qur'anic figures, Abraham exists beyond time and space. The reader does not know where he comes from or where he is bound for. Abraham went through Mecca, where he built the Ka'ba with his son Ishmael; elsewhere he saw the messengers of God going to destroy the city of Lot. Apart from that, he lives at the time of a break between the paganism of his people and the monotheism that he upholds.

The historical aspect of Abraham is thus of little consequence. The Qur'an does not regard him as the father of those who believe in the divine promise. The expression 'Abraham the father of believers' is basically Christian, and I do not know whether it is accepted by Jews who regard Abraham as their father according to the flesh. Muslims, for their part, like to call Abraham the father of the prophets.

He has principally been seen as a champion of monotheism. This is, for example, the theme of a story that is told with great freshness. The future patriarch looks at the stars and wishes to worship one; however, the star disappears. He transfers his attention to the moon and then to the sun, but they too disappear in turn behind the horizon. Abraham understands that none of the stars, subject as they are to change, can be a deity and he turns to the one God (Qur'an 6. 74–83).

Another episode in the saga of Abraham is recounted elsewhere: the destruction of his father's idols. The story is very skilful. After secretly breaking the statues, except for the largest, Abraham puts a rod in the largest statue's hands. When Abraham is accused of the damage, he denies it and maintains that the large statue has broken the others. The people respond, declaring that this is impossible. Here then is proof that they themselves believe the idols to be powerless, as the text concludes or suggests (Qur'an 21. 51–73).

Finally, the Qur'an speaks at some length of Abraham as the forerunner of Islam. It would be wrong to view him as the first Muslim since, from Adam's time, all the righteous are regarded by Islam as Muslims. In any event, he is hailed as the direct forefather of the religious movement launched by Muhammad. The references in Genesis to Abraham settling his son Ishmael in the desert are thus widely repeated and amplified in the Qur'an.

This is shown by a closer examination of a passage on Abraham as the forerunner of Islam in Mecca.

124 And when his Lord tested Abraham by commands, and he fulfilled them, He said, 'Behold, I shall make you a leader [*imām*] for mankind.' Said he, 'And of my offspring?' He said, 'My covenant does not embrace the wrong-doers.'

125 And when We made the House a resort for mankind and a sanctuary, and, 'Take ye the station of Abraham for a place of prayer.' And We commanded Abraham and Ishmael: 'Purify My House for those who circle round it, and those who meditate therein, and those who bow down and prostrate themselves.'

126 And when Abraham said: 'My Lord, make this a land secure, and provide its people with fruits, such of them as believe in God and the Last Day.' He said: 'And whoso disbelieves, to him I shall give enjoyment for a little, then I shall drive him to the torment of the Fire – an evil destination!'

127 And when Abraham, and Ishmael with him, raised up the foundations of the House, 'Our Lord, accept this from us; for Thou art the Hearer, the Knower.

128 O our Lord, make us submissive to Thee, and of our seed a nation submissive to Thee; and show us our rites, and relent towards us; for Thou art the Relentant, the Merciful.

129 O our Lord, raise up among them a Messenger, one of themselves, who shall recite to them Thy signs, and teach them the Book and the Wisdom, and purify them; for Thou art the Mighty, the Wise.'

130 And who but a foolish man would forsake the religion of Abraham? (Qur'an 2. 124–130).

The style of this passage is concise and full of allusions that are sometimes difficult to translate. The rhythm of the sentences, particularly in Arabic, no longer has the breathless quality that is so characteristic of the oldest suras. The present text dates from shortly after the Hijra, the flight to Medina in 622. It is an attempt to influence the Jewish colony in the oasis and, if possible, to win them over.

The extract begins with a reference to Abraham's test. Does this refer to the sacrifice of his son, as one is tempted to believe? The commentators speak of all manner of ritual prescriptions, which shows once again what a very delicate matter it is to interpret these extremely concise texts.

Abraham's historic role is foretold. God will make him an

imām for mankind (v. 124). The title designates the dignitary
who stands in front, who presides and is, by extension, the one
who leads. Abraham is a leader, a model of Islam; others will
follow in his wake. The reference to descendants is harsh: the
promise to choose leaders from among the descendants of
Abraham applies only to the righteous. The sentence therefore
excludes the rest. God's plan here concerns individuals drawn
from the descendants who will be invested with the office of
imām: it does not refer to all the descendants in so far as they
constitute a people.

However, the verse is so short and concise that it is difficult to
elicit the sense without having recourse to the rest of the
doctrine. It says elsewhere that the Children of Israel (hence a
part of the descendants of Abraham) have been the object of
God's preference, but this favour has not made them God's
chosen people in an exclusive sense. The claim of Jews (and
Christians) to be God's chosen people is categorically rejected in
the Qur'an (Qur'an 5. 18).

'O Children of Israel! Remember My favour wherewith I
favoured you, and that I have preferred you above all others'
(Qur'an 2. 122).

But the commentators are quick to observe that this preference was only valid for the past. The Children of Israel were
chosen for their time.

On the other hand, the Qur'an mentions in several places the
gift of prophecy that God poured out upon Abraham's
descendants, especially in Isaac and Jacob's line (cf. Qur'an
6. 89; 29. 27; 57. 26). Abraham, too, appears primarily as the
leader of the biblical prophets and forerunner of the Muslim
community, through his uncompromising monotheistic faith,
good works and prayer. Is not the preference for the Children of
Israel especially evident in this bountiful gift of prophets?

From the following verse (v. 125), the text concentrates on

Abraham, Ishmael and their descendants: in short, it concerns Abraham the ancestor of the Muslims. The Qur'an attributes to him the construction or reconstruction of the Ka'ba, the 'house' of God, to use the classic expression in Semitic languages to designate temples. In Genesis four Palestinian places of worship are linked with the memory of the Patriarch who founded them. It is likely that in Jewish traditions in Arabia a fifth place of worship figured alongside the earlier ones, thus the Ka'ba was associated with the memory of Abraham.

Merely because the Qur'an reports it, this tradition assumes an absolute value for the Muslim. It is held to be certain, without the slightest hesitation, while other popular stories retain a margin of relativity. There is, in fact, a whole literature that places certain events in the Bible in Mecca. It is there that Hagar, dismissed by Sarah, nearly dies of thirst with her child: she is saved by the discovery of the well of Zamzam a few metres from the Ka'ba (cf. Genesis 21. 14–19).

Furthermore, Abraham always appears as the defender of monotheism. Having built the Ka'ba, he purifies it and does not allow it to be defiled by idols. He then proclaims the Muslim pilgrimage (cf. Qur'an 22. 27).

A place called 'the station of Abraham' remains a mystery. Today the name is given to a sort of shrine, quite close to the Ka'ba, where there is a stone bearing Abraham's footprints.

The text traces the origin of the situation in Mecca back to Abraham. The security enjoyed by the inhabitants of this sacred territory, their material resources, the pilgrimage rites, and even, elsewhere, the grace of prayer for their descendants as well as forgiveness on the Day of Judgment, are all the objects of Abraham's requests when he appeals to God (cf. Qur'an 14. 40).

Finally, the last speech concerns Muhammad. As he prays to God to send a Prophet to the Arabs with a scripture and laws that will purify them, Abraham is directly linked to Islam and the Qur'an. Not only the material conditions in Mecca, but even the

Muslim faith, pilgrimage, prayer and the Qur'an, down to the time of the coming of Muhammad, all appear to be the fruit of the intercessions of Abraham.

6

The Prophets Who Were 'Saved'

There are many stories about the prophets in the Qur'an. They are of central importance both for the lessons they embody and for the particular style in which they are written, which makes them accessible to everyone.

First from the point of view of style, these stories use selected historical episodes to illustrate the more theoretical teaching that is given elsewhere. The colourful, concrete character of the narratives makes them easy to grasp and they are stamped on the listeners' memory.

The lessons they provide serve to focus on certain attributes of God, such as His mercy, forgiveness, power to punish, and so on. They reveal nothing essentially new, but they present well-known truths in a much more graphic way. For example, God's goodness manifests itself when the elderly Zechariah begs his Lord for a son despite his advanced age, and his request is granted. God's protection is revealed when His servants are saved from a disaster that destroyed others.

In a sense, in the Qur'an, God reveals Himself through events but His revelation takes up already familiar themes which are stated and restated until the faithful are steeped in them. God reveals Himself through events; can it also be said that He reveals Himself through history? It can and must, but only on condition that it is made quite clear that revelation is not progressive: it constantly returns to the same forgotten truths to remind us of them, or to correct those that have become distorted.

The religious history of the world is, in fact, the history of the prophets, but it is a disjointed history, offering a succession of scenes which are connected neither in time nor space. Only the history of the primitive Muslim community as it was at the time the Qur'an describes it is presented in a more coherent fashion. In both cases, God appears as the master of events. Thus there is this proclamation about the Battle of Badr, in the course of which the Muslims won their first victory against the pagan Meccans (in 624). The text first addresses the Muslims who confronted the Meccans and then Muhammad himself, describing the missiles of war that he used, or rather the symbolic handful of sand that he threw to blind the enemy.

'You did not slay them, but God slew them; and when thou threwest, it was not thyself that threw, but God threw, that He might test the believers by a gracious trial from Himself; verily God is All-Hearing, All-Knowing' (Qur'an 8. 17).

Translations use various words to designate the prophets. Depending on the case, it may be prophet, apostle, messenger or envoy. The reason for this range of terms is that the Arabic of the Qur'an has two different words for them. There is the prophet proper, in the broader sense of the term, i.e. the *nabī*, the old classic word in the Semitic languages. A Muslim tradition lists 124,000 *nabīs* in the religious history of humanity. This type of inspired person is thus relatively widespread. However, Islam has a special category for those prophet-*nabīs* who are also charged with a mission and sent to specific destinations as bearers of a particular message. The prophet-messenger is called the *rasūl* in Arabic and there are only 313 of them. There is, therefore, a superior class of prophet within the mass of inspired persons. They are generally dispatched to a particular people whose language they speak and from whose midst they are drawn. Some have had sacred books to reveal to their kinsmen. Thus Moses was sent to the children of Israel to bring them the

Torah, and Jesus was sent to the same people to bring them the Gospel. Muhammad alone is said to have had a universal mission.

This notion of sending is well known in the Old Testament, where it appears in particular at the inauguration of the great prophets. 'Whom shall I send? Who will go for us?,' says God, in the account of the call of Isaiah (Isaiah 6. 8). This idea is also expressed in the form of an order, as in Moses' call at the Burning Bush: 'I will send thee unto Pharaoh, that thou mayest bring forth my people the children of Israel out of Egypt' (Exodus 3. 10).

The stories of the prophets in the Qur'an vary according to the case, but they are all reminders that God has protected His servants. This protection is only one element in narratives that are crammed with incident. Thus Abraham is saved from the fire into which his people threw him after he destroyed their idols (Qur'an 21. 68–71). Jesus is saved when God miraculously prevents the Jews from crucifying him (Qur'an 4. 157). But in each instance the particular episode is simply mentioned, whereas the text elaborates on many other events in their lives. In the case of Moses, his escape at the crossing of the Red Sea is of more importance, but once again this incident appears among many others. On the other hand, some prophets seem to be mentioned solely in order to recall that God saved them.

The text that we are now going to examine concerns the mission of one of these prophet-messengers. His name is not given: the picture is that of the typical prophet. It will be seen how the doctrine of divine unity is embedded in a whole apologetic context. And, in fact, in many cases, the slights suffered by the various prophets in the Qur'an are exactly the same as those encountered by Muhammad himself among the Quraysh.

The typical prophet and his role in history

31   Then, after them, We produced another generation.

32   And We sent amongst them a Messenger, one of themselves, saying: 'Serve God! You have no other god than He. Will you then not fear Him?'

33   Said the Council of his people who disbelieved, and denied the meeting of the life to come, and to whom We had given ease in the present life: 'This is only a mortal like yourselves, who eats of what you eat and drinks of what you drink.

34   If you obey a mortal like yourselves, then you will surely be losers.

35   Does he promise you that when you are dead, and become dust and bones, you shall be brought forth?

36   Away, away with what you are promised!

37   There is nothing but our present life; we die, and we live, and we shall not be raised again.

38   He is naught but a man who has forged a lie about God, and we will not believe him.'

39   He said: 'O my Lord, help me, for they accuse me of lying.'

40   He said: 'In a little, they will be remorseful!'

41   And the Cry overtook them justly, and We made them as scum; so away then with the wrong-doing people!

42   Then, after them, We produced other generations.

43   No nation can outstrip its term, nor yet delay it.

44   Then We sent Our messengers one after another; whenever its Messenger came to a nation they treated

him as a liar, so We caused them to follow each other, and We made them as but tales; so away with a people who do not believe!

45 Then We sent Moses and his brother Aaron with Our signs and a manifest authority.

46 To Pharaoh and his Council; but they waxed proud, for they were an arrogant people.

47 And they said: 'Shall we believe two mortals like ourselves, whose people are our slaves?'

48 So they treated them as liars, and they were among the destroyed.

49 And We gave Moses the Book, that haply they would be guided.

50 And We made the Son of Mary, and his mother, to be a sign, and gave them refuge upon a height, with a secure abode and a spring (Qur'an 23. 31–50).

In this account, the first thing we notice is a reminder of the succession of prophetic missions. A few verses earlier, the subject was Noah. Here, with the word 'then', the text passes on to the next mission. The commentators note that, in parallel passages, the mission that comes after Noah's is that of Hud, a prophet from South Arabia sent to his people 'Ad, who refused to listen to him. Hud was saved, but his people perished. The reader will find a few details about this people in other stories. The present passage contains no distinctive feature to indicate the historical or geographical context: everything is centred on the essential elements of the scenario, the call to worship one God and the refusal. There are the general characteristics of the prophet-messenger (*rasūl*) that are found everywhere: he is sent to 'his' people from whose bosom God took him. He speaks the language of his people.

The message is summed up here in three points: 1. Worship or serve God (Allah), the one God; 2. Worship none but Him; 3. Fear. Whenever we are faced with Qur'anic texts about the mission of the prophets, it is interesting, in each case, to determine carefully the message that is conveyed. In every instance, we find the centrality of monotheism. For example, note the message expressed in a stereotyped fashion and put into the mouth of different prophets in the Sura of the Poets: 'So fear God, and obey me' (cf. Qur'an 26. 108, 126, 131, etc.). Elsewhere the wording of the message is more explicit: 'Serve God! You have no god other than Him [. . .] Ask forgiveness of your Lord, and turn to Him in repentance' (Qur'an 11. 50, 61, 84). The same formula is used in Sura 7 (cf. Qur'an 7. 59, 65, 73, etc.): 'O my people, serve God! You have no god other than Him . . . '

This faith in the oneness of God, so essential in Islam, is already found in the texts previously examined, notably in the hymn to the Creator in Sura 16. Here it reappears, emphatically proclaimed. Sometimes the messengers have a more limited message. Moses, for example, asks Pharaoh to let the children of Israel go, but the continuation of the story, particularly the discussion with Pharaoh and the conversion of the magicians, reaffirms the idea of the unity of God.

Another characteristic feature of the prophet-messenger, which is absolutely clear in most cases, is merely suggested here. The prophet-messenger announces that if people refuse to believe and obey his message, a terrible punishment will descend upon them. If, on the other hand, they believe and obey, they will enjoy ineffable bliss. Hence the two terms that are generally applied to the Messengers, *nadhīr* (one who warns against a catastrophe that he announces), and *bashīr* (one who proclaims good news). Muhammad himself is called by both names, for his message promises paradise to the good and hell to the wicked. Here the text merely says: 'Fear'. The absence of a direct object makes it possible to assume either the fear of God or the fear of punishment, or perhaps both.

Immediately after the message comes the argument. This typical outline of the hostility encountered by the prophet reflects Muhammad's own situation at the time. The reference to a 'council' primarily concerns the people of 'Ad; but it reminded contemporaries that the council of Elders in Mecca had shown the same opposition to Muhammad.

The threefold reproach addressed to opponents consists of:

a reproach for calling the resurrection and the realities of the afterlife a lie;

a reproach for allowing themselves to be seduced by the comforts of this life;

a reproach for not believing in the mission of the prophet who speaks to them.

The denial of the afterlife is perfectly clear here; it is repeated to reinforce the affirmation. It is the same great objection that the pagan Arabs made to Muhammad. Thus opponents would deliberately reduce the prophets to the level of ordinary men in order to reject their claims.

Note, from the point of view of style, the formulae which avoid going into detail so as not to distract attention from the principal centre of interest: 'He eats of what you eat and drinks of what you drink.'

By way of contrast, the phrase 'If you obey a mortal like yourselves, then you will surely be losers . . . ' calls attention to an essential Qur'anic position. 'You will be losers,' say the leaders of the opposition. The Muslim who knows his Qur'an immediately thinks that, on the contrary, it is those who do not follow the Prophet who will be 'losers'. The word 'losers' is pronounced: it hovers briefly before swooping down upon those who will be the real losers. The ground is prepared to dispose the listener to accept what follows.

For, in truth, a sense of impending danger is in the air. There is, in fact, a law that could be called the great Qur'anic law of

world history. The word law is not in the Qur'an but the
expression used, 'the way of God', amounts to the same thing. It
describes the immutable way in which God acts. This way (or
law) operates in the following manner: nations hostile to the
Messengers of God are always destroyed; and when destruction
comes, the small number of people who are saved consists of
those who believe and obey the Prophet.

How often the Qur'an refers to this way of God! It does seem
that some such argument played an important part in the
preaching of Islam in the Meccan period. Confronted by the
Meccans who refuse to believe in the authenticity of Muhammad's prophetic mission, the Qur'an recalls that all the earlier
prophets were exposed to similar rejection by their people.
By identifying Muhammad's situation with that of previous
prophets, the text gives special prominence to these stories of
the past. They are not only about Noah and Moses, but about
contemporary figures as well. When the Qur'an recalls the Flood
or the drowning of the Egyptians in the Red Sea and the fate of
the inhabitants of Sodom and Gomorrah (called the cities of Lot
in the Qur'an), it threatens the Meccans who refuse to believe in
Muhammad with the same fate. In fact this warning is plainly
stated on several occasions (cf. Qur'an 73. 15–18, where, after
a reminder of the fate met by Moses' Pharaoh, the text threatens
those who do not believe in the Qur'an with hell). But the same
warning exists implicitly in all the accounts of the prophets of
punishment.

The law itself is presented as an obvious fact, affirmed with the
whole authority of the Qur'an, while at the same time going back
in essence to classic religious traditions in some Jewish and
Christian circles. This lesson from the past, together with the
punishment of the guilty angels, the drowning of Noah's
contemporaries, and the destruction of Sodom and Gomorrah,
is mentioned in the Second Epistle of Peter 2. 4–10 in the New
Testament (cf. also the Epistle of Jude, verses 6–7). The Qur'an
interrogates the reader. Did he not pass in his caravan near the

places where the Thamud, the people of the prophet Salih, were destroyed for their unbelief? And do not the ruins of the town of al-Hijr (in Arabia: cf. the title of Sura 15), which is now called Meda'in Salih, the cities of Salih, recall this people's fate? As it urges readers to open their eyes and take note of this particular case, the Qur'an implies that the cause of the ruins is obvious:

'Travel in the land, and see what has been the end of the guilty' (Qur'an 27. 69).

'And thou shalt not find any change in the way of God. Have they not travelled in the land and seen what was the end of those before them, though mightier than they in power?' (Qur'an 35. 42–43).

A similar argument must have struck the Israelites when, as their caravans made their way through the depression of the Dead Sea, in the midst of the desert, they came upon blocks that recalled the transformation of Lot's wife into a pillar of salt (cf. Genesis 19. 26).

But to return to the present text: what follows is as simple as what has gone before. The prophet appeals to God and the readers are reassured: they know that the wicked are going to be punished. The text tells them so: 'In a little, they will be remorseful!' The final catastrophe is barely mentioned here. We guess that it will entail destruction.

Then the history of the prophet-messengers continues. It is not a history of revelation, for the core of the essential doctrinal truths always remains the same. It is not a factual history: there are news flashes of selected episodes in the lives of successive prophets, connected as they are here, by the conjunction 'then'.

The affirmation of the omnipotence of God is repeated in a context of fact. No community can alter its ordained fate. In this passage, the missions of Moses and Jesus are barely mentioned.

A later chapter will be devoted to Jesus and the Christians.

Unfortunately we can only give some general information here about the other prophets cited.

We will confine ourselves to those who could be called 'prophets who were saved', rather than prophets of punishment or prophets linked with the destruction of a people. The Qur'an mentions them to illustrate the great Qur'anic law of history that is referred to above. Six prophet-messengers (three from the Bible and three from Arabia who are not mentioned in the Bible) appear in this context. The Qur'an often brackets them together in the same group. Sometimes there is only a series of short descriptions of each of them. Take, for example, the passage in Sura 51 where, after describing the scene in which the messengers of God announce the birth of a son to Abraham, the text goes on at once to the destruction of the city where Lot lived and then to the conflict between Moses and Pharaoh; finally there are the disasters that destroyed the peoples of 'Ad, Thamud and Noah, all of whom refused to listen to the Messenger of God who came to them (cf. Qur'an 51.31–46). The same list is found again in Qur'an 22.42–48.

On the other hand, there can be a much more detailed treatment of these crises, as in Suras 26, 7 or 11. In one respect, Moses fits into the category of 'prophets who were saved', with the episode of the Red Sea from which he emerges unscathed, while Pharaoh and his soldiers meet their death. However, Moses' personality by far transcends this particular incident. His portrait has a special place in the Qur'an. In fact Moses is the prophet to whom the greatest number of Qur'anic verses are dedicated. In Mecca he is undeniably in the forefront. In Medina, he yields pride of place to Abraham, for at that time the texts lay emphasis on Islam as a return to the religion of Abraham; but Moses still figures prominently in the suras of the period. Whenever the Qur'an wishes to move or to rebuke the Jews of Medina, it reminds them of how their ancestors were rebellious when Moses led them out of Egypt and guided them in the desert.

A few words about each of these 'prophets who were saved' will help the reader to place them when he comes across references to them in the text.

First of all, there are the three prophet-messengers from Arabia, Hud, Salih and Shu'ayb of Midian. In Sura 26 (verses 123–191) these three prophets are presented in a stereotyped outline, with the same message and almost the same words. Only a few details about their country and the activities of their countrymen make it possible to identify them. One is reminded of the statues in medieval cathedrals whose faces, figures and features are all similar: there is nothing to distinguish one saint from another. A single attribute is there to make an identification possible: for example, the keys of St Peter, the sword of St Paul, the shell or the pilgrim's staff of St James, and so on. Similarly, in the Qur'an, were it not for a few details about their people (they hewed out houses from the mountains, built castles on hills, engaged in trade, etc.), these prophets would be indistinguishable from one another.

Hud addresses shepherds and farmers in South Arabia: we are not told the reason for his people's disobedience.

Shu'ayb is presented as an inhabitant of the country of Midian, south of the Gulf of Aqaba, on the Red Sea, a hive of commercial activity. It appears that texts in which he is not named must be related to him, but in Suras 26, 7 and 11 his name is clearly stated. Elsewhere there is some doubt.

Salih addresses the people of Thamud, known in the history of Arabia for their rock inscriptions and archaeological remains. In the Qur'an, Salih's prophetic message concerns a sacred camel to which the people were commanded to give a share of the water. It was a time of drought, the people refused to obey, killed the camel and were almost immediately destroyed by divine punishment.

These must have been old Arabian traditions which the Qur'an has taken up and used as arguments to reinforce the authority of the prophets.

In the case of the Bible, the stories of Noah and the Flood, the destruction of the city of Lot and the drowning of Pharaoh in the Red Sea are too well known for it to be necessary to go over them.

The role of Moses, on the other hand, must be further stressed in order to convey his importance in the Qur'an and to persuade readers to immerse themselves in the relevant texts. Not only is Moses the Old Testament character to whom the greatest number of verses in the Qur'an are devoted, but he is also the one whose portrayal in the Qur'an is closest to that in the Bible, despite certain silences. The reader will find Moses depicted in long passages in the following suras: Ta Ha (Qur'an 20. 9–98), The Poets (Qur'an 26. 10·68), The Story (Qur'an 28, 3–43), The Heights (Qur'an 7. 103–155), The Cow (Qur'an 2. 49–74), etc.

In addition to the theme of God's protection of His messenger whom He sustains and helps to triumph, and to whom He gives the Tablets of the Law, the theme of the liberation of an oppressed people is plainly emphasized on several occasions. In the Qur'anic text presented and commented on in this chapter, Pharaoh already refers to the bondage of the Hebrew people. This idea appears clearly in the verse:

'But We desired to show favour to those who were oppressed in the land, and to make them leaders, and to make them heirs' (Qur'an 28. 5).

A striking fact emerges when we look at history. Whenever a political religious movement (more or less faithful to the Bible) has sought liberation from a position of inferiority or the seizure of power, the figure of Moses is almost always in the forefront. This is still the case with twentieth-century prophetic movements of anti-colonial origin. Moses is the epitome of the political religious prophet.

The reader who is conversant with the Pentateuch will find many familiar scenes, but they are presented in a different way and bear the stamp of the Qur'an's style: interludes proclaiming monotheism appear here and there. Moses' father is not named: the name 'Imran in the Qur'an designates the father of Mary, the mother of Jesus. It resembles the name Amram, Moses' father in the Bible, but it appears only in passing and plays no part in the text. This, once again, seeks to impart lessons and not to reconstruct history for its own sake. Mary, Aaron's sister in the Bible, does not appear in the Qur'an and it is Mary, the mother of Jesus, who is called Aaron's sister (Qur'an 19. 28), again in passing and without any importance being attached to it. Muslims who appreciate the difficulty which this poses respond by taking the word sister in the wider sense of the term, as if it were 'Mary, of Aaron's line'.

At the scene of the Golden Calf, a mysterious character appears: he is called the Samaritan (*al-Sāmirī*). It is hard to know what this word signifies. Some Westerners have seen a connection with the golden calves of Samaria, but this would take us several centuries beyond Moses. In the absence of other documents, one is very hesitant to subscribe to such a hypothesis (cf. Qur'an 20. 85–95).

Aaron's attitude in the episode of the Golden Calf is not clear. The elusive nature of the style provides too few explicit details for it to be possible to reconstruct his role (Qur'an 20. 92–94). Later Muslim tradition states that Aaron could not possibly have behaved with the Golden Calf in the way that is described in the text of the Pentateuch, for a prophet is *a priori* sinless and infallible.

In the Qur'an, the circumstances of Moses' birth are identical to those described in the Bible, but there is much less detail. The measures taken by the Egyptians against the Hebrews decreed that newborn males should be put to death, while girl babies were spared. Moses is abandoned on the river and taken in by Pharaoh's wife (not his daughter, as in the Book of Exodus). The miraculous aspect is magnified. God dries up the milk of all the wet-nurses to whom the child is entrusted. Finally he is given back to his mother to nurse after a clever intervention by his older sister.

Moses' murder of the Egyptian is presented more as a sin than as a prelude to a liberation movement (Qur'an 28. 15–16, 33). All the delicacy of the biblical scenes of idylls at the fountain or well is centred here on Moses. In the Qur'an there is nothing about Eliezer and Rebecca or Jacob's return to Mesopotamia. It is Moses who waters the flocks belonging to two defenceless young girls from the land of Midian where he has just arrived. Finally he marries the eldest, who has arranged for her father to invite him (Qur'an 28. 22–29).

The burning bush, the signs of the rod that turns into a serpent and the white hand, Aaron's role as his close aide, the mission to beg Pharaoh to let the Hebrew people go, Pharaoh's refusal, the magicians, the plagues of Egypt, the crossing of the Red Sea, the Tablets of the Law, the covenant at Sinai, the Golden Calf, the quail and manna, the water from the rock, the promised land (without labouring the point), the Hebrews' refusal to fight: all these episodes appear in one form or another. Finally Moses receives the Torah.

The tone of the suras varies according to the period. In Medina (in Sura 2), the Qur'an begins by calling on the Jews to come over to Islam. The problem arose because, although there were few if any Jews living in Mecca, their community in Medina was substantial, representing half the population of the oasis. In order to move them, the Qur'an in Medina repeats the benefits that God formerly bestowed on Moses. Then, faced with their continued rejection, it confronts them with their ancestors' hardness of heart and hesitance to have faith in Moses, and suggests that they have an attitude which is as reprehensible today as it was at the time of the Exodus.

'Then your hearts became hardened thereafter and are like

rocks, or even harder; for there are rocks from which rivers gush forth, and others split asunder, so that water issues from them, and others fall down through fear of God' (Qur'an 2. 74).

Thus Moses appears to many Muslims as the prophet who was confronted by a trying, troublesome people who rebelled. This idea, consistent with the depiction of Moses in the Medinan suras, has been reinforced once again by events in Palestine and the conviction that the people of Israel refuse to submit to God's plan.

Other points still remain to be indicated. A famous prayer of Moses in the Qur'an, in which he asks God to see Him, has given rise to a number of mystical commentaries (Qur'an 7. 143).

An examination of the Qur'anic texts on Moses should also elicit the motives Pharaoh gives for rejecting Moses' mission. Some complaints, like the accusation made to Moses that he wished to chase the Egyptians out of their country (Qur'an 20. 57), call for an explanation. Is this an echo of the conflict between the Hyksos and later dynasties? Or simply a projection into the past of the situation in Mecca with the Meccans' fear of the growing power of the Muslims?

As it is impossible to dwell on everything, we will note only three other passages that present distinctive features.

First, there is a long narrative about Moses (a completely different Moses from the one in the Bible) travelling with a supernatural figure. This narrative is a kind of moral fable showing that events in life which are often incomprehensible to us are perfectly ordered towards a providential end that is beyond our understanding (Qur'an 18, 60–82).

Then there is a passage about Pharaoh, with some elegiac verses on his death. This elegy is a rare example of this literary form in the Qur'an, if not the only one (Qur'an 44. 17–33).

Finally, there is the passage in which Pharaoh is associated with Haman and Korah in the rejection of Moses' message

(Qur'an 40. 23–45). Korah appears elsewhere in the Qur'an (Qur'an 28. 76–82) and the earth swallows him up. The reason is no longer directly linked to prophecy as in the Bible, where Korah and his companions reject the pre-eminence of Moses and Aaron in the name of the sacred character of the people of God. They set the community against individual charisms (Numbers 16. 3). Here Korah is the fabulously rich man whose wealth has made him proud in the sight of God. Haman's name is quite familiar in the Bible, but it appears in the Book of Esther in an entirely different context. Here Pharaoh, after speaking of killing Moses, asks Haman to build him a high tower so that he can ascend to the God of Moses (cf. v. 36). Could this be a vague recollection of the pyramids?

So far Muslim exegesis has paid hardly any attention to this confusion of names. Anti-Muslim polemical literature has not failed to raise the point, and it is probable that the Jewish opposition in Medina at the time of the Prophet was quick to speak out. On the Muslim side, critics have either behaved as if nothing were amiss or else they have thought that it was a case of different individuals sharing the same name. In 1947, a doctoral thesis presented at the University of Cairo by an assistant to the professor of Qur'anic exegesis sought to face the difficulty and resolve it by putting forward the idea of literary forms in the Qur'an, with different kinds of truth according to the form. It suggested that the Pharaoh-Haman block may have been deliberately intended. To give more force to the style and to show what opposition Moses faced, the Qur'an, it was said, linked two biblical characters who had lived in different times and places. The conjunction of the arch-tyrant, Pharaoh, with the typical unjust minister, Haman, symbolized the strength of the opposition to the prophet. This view was violently rejected by Egyptians at the time.

However, once again, we must not forget that many readers of the Qur'an do not seek to reconstruct the narratives as a whole. Most of them follow its recitation as a way of being in the

presence of God, of being blessed, and they frequently remember a simple isolated phrase that sustains their meditation.
It is often a beautiful detail or an uplifting thought that sticks in
their mind. It is said, for example, that the great Islamic thinker,
Shah Waliullah (eighteenth century), born in Delhi, was profoundly moved by God's words to Moses:

'I have chosen thee for Myself' (Qur'an 20. 41).

In short, we are faced with a series of episodes, many of them
already known from the Bible, which are recapitulated in the
Qur'anic perspective of the glorification of divine unity and
majesty. Many of the nuances and many of the conclusions are
not the same, but more importantly, an element that is essential
in the Bible is no longer present. The Moses of the Bible stands
in the line of God's promise to Abraham and the election of a
particular people. Neither the promise nor the election appears
in the Qur'an. This alone is enough to give sacred history a
totally different direction from that in the Bible.

7

Jesus, Son of Mary

To speak of Jesus in the Qur'an is, first of all, to speak of a prophet. Although he is designated by titles that are conferred on him alone and considered to be one of the greatest prophets sent to mankind, the equal of Abraham, Moses or even Muhammad, nevertheless he remains one of the prophets, all of whom are equally respected by the Muslim.

'The Messenger believes in what was sent down to him from his Lord, as do the believers also; each one believes in God and His angels, and in His Books and His Messengers; we make no distinction between any of His Messengers' (Qur'an 2. 285).

Certain characteristics are in fact common to all these men of God, characteristics that sometimes appear clearly and are sometimes implicit in all that is said about them. The prophets are first and foremost Muslims, and their conduct is an illustration of Islam. They preach monotheism and stand before God as model believers. Thus Abraham dissociates himself from paganism to turn to the one God:

'[They whom you worship] are an enemy to me, except the Lord of the Worlds, who created me, and Himself guides me, who gives me food and drink, and when I am sick, heals me, who will cause me to die, and then bring me to life, and who, I

hope, will forgive me my faults on the Day of Judgment'
(Qur'an 26. 77–82).

Jesus, for his part, is a true Muslim with his filial devotion and
his sense of prayer and almsgiving. He describes his mission
thus:

'I am the servant of God; He has given me the Book, and
made me a Prophet, and He has made me blessed wherever I
may be; and He has enjoined upon me prayer and almsgiving,
so long as I live, and to be dutiful towards my mother; and He
has not made me arrogant, wretched. Peace be upon me, the
day I was born, the day I die, and the day I shall be raised to
life!' (Qur'an 19. 30–33).

The same holds true for Job, the model of steadfastness. In the
case of Solomon, the jinn and the Queen of Sheba, the Qur'an
relates a whole collection of stories, marked by a profusion of
the miraculous, which are unknown in the Bible, and finally
Solomon takes the opportunity to thank God for all His blessings
(Qur'an 27. 19).

The actual style and drift of the Qur'an give a very distinctive
flavour to the narratives about the prophets. Their conciseness
means that descriptions are reduced to essentials and only
certain facts are emphasized; hence there is a simplification that
gives the text clarity and force. On the other hand, psychological
factors are over-simplified: subtleties disappear, as everything
goes back to the natural attitude of the religious man before
God. The story of Job occupies three verses in the Qur'an while,
in the Old Testament, the cycle of poems with the prologue and
conclusion covers forty chapters. From the Bible, there remains
the description of Job's suffering, his edifying submission and
final reward. It was the Devil who touched him. But all the
original features of the biblical Job, with his complaints and his

question to God (Why do you make me suffer when I have not sinned?), have disappeared.

In the same way Jesus describes his mission in terms of the most ordinary religious experience. There are statements of a general nature, expressing basic truths, without any hint of the originality of the Gospel message. Only the allusion to Mary makes it clear that it has to do with Jesus.

Finally, the prophet represents an example of human perfection that in principle rules out any idea of the fall, even as a starting point for the finest example of repentance. Adam sins, Moses kills the Egyptian ... that is almost all that is said in black and white about the lapses of the men of God. Take the cases of David and the litigants, although followed by an appeal for forgiveness (Qur'an 38. 21–26), and Aaron and the Golden Calf, although followed by Moses' words of reproach to his brother (Qur'an 20. 92–94). However much these incidents may remind the reader of the Bible of the episode of David and Bathsheba or the events at Sinai, the Muslim relies on the terseness and silences of the Qur'an and rejects any exegesis that would impute grave offences to the sinless, infallible prophets. When David asks for and receives divine forgiveness in the Qur'an, it is to pause very briefly, without dismissing it immediately, over the mere idea of such a sin.

Hence the moral, edifying aspect of these Qur'anic stories. There is nothing comparable to the impact of their biblical counterparts in which the faithful are confronted with human reality, with its good and bad sides, the contrast of passion and faith and, finally, the need for redemption and deliverance which the Old Testament inspires in men's hearts. On the other hand, precisely because he views things from a totally different perspective, the Muslim is deeply shocked when he finds stories in the Bible that are all too human. The David of the Bible and the David in the Qur'an belong to two different worlds.

The stories about the prophets play yet another role in the Qur'an. The fact that Muhammad speaks of these far-off events, when he himself was not an eyewitness, is stressed. The text thus suggests that he could only have known of them through revelation. Hence the apologetic note that pervades the stories. Take, for example, this dictum in the Qur'an which is addressed to Muhammad about a well-known incident in the Infancy Gospels. Lots are drawn to ascertain who will take charge of Mary:

'This is of the tidings of things unseen, that We reveal to thee; for thou wast not with them, when they cast lots with reeds [pens] which of them should have charge of Mary; nor wast thou with them when they were disputing' (Qur'an 3. 44).

In the Protevangelium of James, the High Priest summons all the widowers of Judaea so that one of them can take care of Mary. Mary has grown up and can no longer stay in the temple where she has been living. Each brings a rod: the one from whose rod a dove emerges will be chosen. The miracle takes place with Joseph's rod. In the Qur'an none of this is explicit.

Whatever may be the details of these stories, their presence poses a problem: that of the historical relationship between the Qur'anic text and other earlier texts. This question, which is raised by Western exegetes about all religious works, including the books of the Bible, is not yet admissible in studies of Muslim exegesis. The theology of revelation, the descent of a text transmitted from heaven complete to the last detail, was the theology of the rabbis in the first centuries of our era; Christian circles adopted it for a long period and it is still the most commonly held official Muslim doctrine. Only a few isolated voices are trying to widen the discussion. For the present, however, the fact that the Qur'anic stories had been previously known, either in the canonical books or in apocryphal texts, has no importance in the face of the official doctrine. God who is all-powerful is free to repeat anything He pleases.

Jesus in the Qur'an has his own distinctive features. And it is through the passages devoted to him in the Qur'an that the whole Muslim world sees him. The Qur'anic view is still the inspiration for virtually all writers. Thus a work on Jesus that recently appeared in Egypt begins with a chapter entitled 'The Jesus of History' which contains nothing but Qur'anic verses. The writer then explains them for two or three pages, reminding us that, for the Muslim, the Qur'an is the most reliable, indeed the only reliable, document on the subject. Only then does the author turn to consider the Jesus of the Councils, the Jesus of the Gospels and of present-day Christians.

The principal texts on Jesus and Mary are Qur'an 19. 16–40, with the Annunciation, Christmas, the return of Mary and the child to their people and the response of the child Jesus to criticisms addressed to his mother. The whole section concludes with a theological precision that appears to belong to a later period. In Qur'an 3. 33–61, we have the birth of Mary, her childhood, Zechariah and his son, and then the long passage translated below. In Sura 4, verse 157 describes the crucifixion and, in verses 171–172, the person of Jesus is defined quite explicitly. There are also many other passages to be noted.

Jesus and Mary

42 And when the angels said, 'O Mary! God has chosen thee, and purified thee; He has chosen thee above the women of the worlds [. . .].'

45 When the angels said, 'O Mary! God gives thee good tidings of a Word from Him whose name is the Messiah, Jesus, son of Mary, illustrious in this world and the next, and one of those brought near.

46 He shall speak to men in the cradle, and as a grown man, and he shall be one of the righteous.'

47 'My Lord,' said Mary, 'how shall I have a son, seeing no

man has touched me?' He said: 'Even so, God creates what He will. When He decrees a thing, He does but say to it, "Be", and it is.'

48 And He will teach him the Book, the Wisdom, the Torah and the Gospel;

49 And he shall be a Messenger to the Children of Israel saying, 'I have come to you with a sign from your Lord. I will create for you out of clay the likeness of a bird; then I will breathe into it, and it will become a bird, by God's leave. And I will heal the blind and the leper, and bring the dead to life, by God's leave. I shall announce to you what you may eat and what you may store up in your houses. Surely in that is a sign for you, if you are believers.

50 Likewise confirming the truth of the Torah that is before me, and to make lawful to you certain things which were forbidden to you. I have come to you with a sign from your Lord; so fear God, and obey me.

51 Surely God is my Lord and your Lord; so worship Him. This is a straight path.'

52 And when Jesus perceived their unbelief, he said, 'Who will be my helpers in the cause of God?' The disciples said, 'We will be helpers of God; we believe in God, and bear thou witness that we are Muslims (have surrendered).

53 O our Lord, we believe in what Thou hast sent down, and we follow the Messenger. So write us down with those who bear witness.'

54 And they plotted, and God plotted, and God is the best of plotters.

55 When God said, 'O Jesus, I will take thee and raise thee to Myself, and I will purify thee of those who believe not.

I will set those who follow thee above those who
disbelieve until the Day of Resurrection. Then unto Me
shall you return, and I will judge between you wherein
you differ' (Qur'an 3. 42–55).

Mary is 'chosen' by God. The notion of choice occurs several
times in the Qur'an; it goes with the notions of God's omnipotence, His mercy and the gratuitousness of His gifts. The scope of
this choice is defined by the context, and when the Qur'an says
'above the women of the worlds', the expression recalls the
favours granted to the Children of Israel who were formerly the
chosen people in the world.

The graces bestowed on Mary appear at her birth: her mother
placed her (with Jesus) under God's protection against Satan. A
tradition even maintains that Satan, who touches all human
beings and so makes newborn babies cry, touched neither Jesus
nor Mary. The graces appear in the account of Mary's childhood
in the temple in Jerusalem (cf. Qur'an 3. 35–41, so similar to
texts in the Protevangelium of James).

Muslim exegesis lays particular stress on the miracle of Jesus'
birth without a father, analogous to the creation of Adam
without a father and a proof of divine omnipotence. It also
stresses that Mary, together with Pharaoh's wife, is given as an
example of the virtuous Muslim woman by the Qur'an itself
(Qur'an 66. 11–12).

Her purity is affirmed in a categorical fashion which the
commentators explain in different ways, ranging from physio-
logical considerations to recognition of the 'immaculate' nature
of Mary.

The annunciation in verse 45 above should be compared with
the annunciation in Qur'an 19. 16–21. In the latter passage, the
Angel is called 'Our spirit', that is, Gabriel, since for Muslims
the term spirit always denotes a spiritual being. Neither date nor
place is specified. The East, the desert, a palm tree, a stream, is
all. Everything centres on the miracle of the virgin birth and the

divine protection against hunger, thirst and the calumnies of those around. In Christian tradition, the palm tree appears not at the birth but at the later time of the flight into Egypt, at least in the Gospel of Pseudo-Matthew, Chapter 20. A tired Mary rests in the desert in the shade of a palm tree. She desires some of its fruit; the child Jesus, who is two years old, orders the tree to bend down and then to rise up and open its roots. A hidden spring appears and water gushes forth for Mary and Joseph to drink. Then, according to the same popular Christian tradition, a branch of the said palm tree is transplanted to heaven to provide the deserving elect with palms of victory. But let us return to the Qur'an.

One of Jesus' miracles is to speak in the cradle to refute the calumnies against his mother. This idea has had a profound effect on the Muslim mentality, and to slander a virtuous Muslim woman is still considered one of the greatest sins. The text has certainly contributed to the preservation of the sense of woman's honour in Muslim society.

The miracle of the virgin birth itself is compared in the Qur'an to an act of creation. When God commands something to be, it is. This is the creative *fiat* (cf. Qur'an 3. 47, 59). Hence Muslims' standard explanation of Jesus' title 'The Word of God', or 'Speech of God', by the idea that he was created by a word of God.

In verse 45 in our passage, the names given to Jesus and to no other prophet in the Qur'an are particularly to be noted. He is, first of all, the Messiah. In fact the commentators provide a whole series of explanations of this title, but they make little of the historical aspect of messianism. This aspect is not unknown, but it is lost among others. The most obvious result of the presence of this title is a break with Judaism. Islam is at variance with Judaism because of both its respect for Mary's virginity and its theoretical recognition of Jesus' messiahship.

The Qur'anic name for Jesus ('Isa) is not the name given to him by Arab Christians (Yasu'). The origin of this name poses a problem: it appears to have been used before Islam only by the Mandaean sect, a few thousand of whom still live in the marshes of Lower Iraq. Various explanations have been proposed. It would take too long to reproduce them here and none of them is conclusive. It is better to bear in mind an undeniable truth. The traveller in exclusively Muslim countries, in whole areas of which Christians can be counted on the fingers of one hand, is impressed by the fact that everything the populace knows about Jesus and Mary comes from the Qur'an and Muslim traditions. It is 'Isa who is known and not Jesus. There is still this mystery of a personal relationship that transcends all the over-intellectual studies.

The word 'illustrious' is an honorific title that is interpreted in different ways.

In the Qur'an, those brought near to God form a well-defined category of beings consisting of the elect and the angels.

Finally, the title 'Word' (or 'Speech'), needs to be carefully considered. In this sura, Jesus is said to be *a* word from God. But this term, which is still relative, is strengthened elsewhere when the Qur'an calls Jesus '*His* word' (or His speech), i.e. *the* word or speech of God that He conveyed to Mary (Qur'an 4. 171). In this last passage, Jesus is also said to be *a* spirit from God. The reader must excuse my emphasis on the definite and indefinite articles; too often Christians confuse the two and speak of Jesus as the spirit of God. The expression is not Qur'anic; once again he is *a* spirit from God.

The Qur'an compares Jesus' case with Adam's: both were created without fathers. But the parallel between them is not complete in the Qur'an, where Adam is never called Word of God.

Jesus was sent to the Children of Israel (v. 49). Thus in the eyes of Muslims his mission is limited in time and space. Muhammad alone has a mission that is universal and valid until the end of time.

Jesus received the Scripture; the book that is particularly associated with him is the Gospel. But here again there is a misunderstanding with Christians. Just as the icons which many Arab travellers would have seen in the Eastern churches represented Christ and the twelve apostles as each carrying a book, so Jesus in the Qur'an is depicted as one who received a book from God. The conception of the Gospel is a sensitive subject in Christian-Muslim relations: it must be considered in connection with passages in which the Qur'an asserts that Jews and Christians have distorted the texts of their scriptures. But the problem of the scope of this accusation is too vast to be dealt with here. Is it an accusation addressed to a small group, or one directed at all the Jews and Christians in the entire world? Does it concern a falsification of the text itself, or only tendentious interpretations of a text that remains authentic? It is enough here to point out that the problem exists and that it is important.

Jesus' miracles are also of importance (v. 49). A simple Muslim once told me that when the preacher at the mosque speaks of Jesus, it is usually to emphasize his miracles. The Qur'an gives hardly any details about them. Some of the miracles can be found in the Infancy Gospels, for example, the raising from the dead, while others, like the healing of the blind and the leper, do not appear. The clay bird that Jesus brings to life is well known in Western iconography; it comes from the Infancy Gospel known by the name of Thomas, which is different from the other Gospel of Thomas, the Gnostic work that has aroused much interest. It must be noted that all the miracles are worked 'by God's leave'.

The support that Jesus has from his disciples who fight for him is in the tradition of the triumph of the prophets (v. 52). Elsewhere in the Qur'an it is written that the duty of holy war is recorded in the Gospel as it is in the Torah and the Qur'an. In spite of the surprise of Christians, who find nothing of the sort in the Gospels they possess, this statement presents no difficulty for believers: since the Qur'an says so, it must be true (Qur'an 9. 111). In short, the disciples believe, obey and help their master to victory. The puzzle of God's plotting in response to man's plotting is found elsewhere in the Qur'an.

The death of Jesus raises a serious problem. Many Muslims, relying on a verse that says that the Jews 'neither killed, nor crucified Jesus', think that after his condemnation to death Jesus was miraculously raised to heaven. A double was substituted for him and crucified in his place (Qur'an 4. 157). The Qur'anic wording that describes this event is highly allusive. Some have suggested taking the statement in a figurative sense, as if it said: they have not got the better of him, they have not destroyed him, since he is still alive. Here verse 55 speaks of Jesus whom God 'has taken to Himself'. Does this refer to his death, since the Arabic expression 'take to Himself' which is put into God's mouth generally means to cause to die? Or is this a recall without death, which is possible too, as the word is also used for occasions when God takes souls in sleep and then returns them the next morning? Both explanations are grammatically possible.

To complete what is said about Christianity, it is necessary to draw attention to passages like Qur'an 4. 171, where it is written 'Say not, "Three",' and others in which Muslims have generally found a denial of the divinity of Christ, although some contemporary Christian thinkers are trying to show the possibility of another exegesis.

Jesus appears as the leader of the Christians. The latter have received from him kindness and forbearance, and the monastic life is attributed to them (Qur'an 57. 27). The emphasis is no longer the same as in the Gospels. The expectation of the Jewish people, the Roman occupation, the weight of sin and the desire for deliverance are not mentioned. Nor is there any question of a saviour or cross. And even Joseph, by his absence, removes a reason for human concern. Joseph's discovery of Mary's condition would provide an element of drama. Here everything is the gift of God and opponents are reduced to silence by the miracle of the child who speaks and the action of the disciples. The human, historical aspect gives way to a supernatural vision of things, while the values common to all religions are emphasized.

The reference to the 'covenant' God made with the Jews and Christians is worth noting (Qur'an 5. 12–14). It would be interesting for the reader to examine these three verses closely. The content of the past covenant with the Children of Israel appears here. God promises to be with them if they practise prayer and almsgiving and if they help the Messengers of God and finance their struggle. If they do this, God will grant them forgiveness and bring them to paradise. The assistance to the Messengers engaged in the struggle is a direct reference to the contemporary context of the preaching of this sura. Muhammad never accepted the fact that the Jews (those in Medina and in the oases of the north) not only did not help him but even sought to establish contact with his enemies. And he made them pay for it dearly.

At all events, these requirements correspond exactly to the demands made of the Arab tribes that came to join him: ritual prayer, a financial contribution intended to cover the expenses of administration and charity and, finally, support in the struggle. What remains from the Old Testament? The fundamental religious principles that are common to all monotheisms.

Immediately after this reference to the covenant, the text emphasizes the division among Christians that is attributed to a punishment from God. The spectacle of this division is an argument against them. Is it perhaps even, in practice, the most powerful argument of all (Qur'an 5. 14)? The Qur'an adds that, in view of this state of affairs, Muhammad has also been sent to the Jews and Christians who have lost sight of their ideals (cf. Qur'an 5. 19). And elsewhere it affirms that the coming of Muhammad was foretold by the Torah and the

Gospel (Qur'an 7. 157) and even announced by Jesus (Qur'an 61. 6). These last assertions have been the source of lengthy polemics with Jews and Christians.

8

The Muslim Community

The text of the Qur'an that will be presented in this chapter is an appeal to Muslims to unite and form a body that will be true to their communal vocation. Before broaching the subject, some indication will be given of the line to be taken. In the previous chapters, readers who are conversant with the biblical traditions will have found many landmarks that enabled them to get their bearings; they are now going to enter an entirely different world.

In fact the Qur'an preserves a large number of texts that describe the first Muslim community, its formation and consolidation. Some contain simple allusions, others mention an event or a proper name, but most of the time they consist of orders, exhortations and particular decisions that take on their full meaning only when placed in their historical context.

The Muslim ideal has appeared up to this point as trusting submission to the Lord and Creator of the world who is master of history. The great prophet-messengers were entrusted with missions, each to his own nation. They tried to weld their people into a community and more or less succeeded. Noah and Lot were heeded only by their families and, even then, the former's son and latter's wife failed to do exactly as they were told and perished. On the other hand, Moses was able to lead the Hebrews, while Jesus was followed by the Christians. And, at the time of Muhammad, the two large biblical communities in Arabia and the neighbouring countries were still the Jews and the Christians. The first Muslim community appears from the very beginning in a biblical context.

Specialists have discussed at great length whether Islam should be viewed primarily as a movement akin to Judaism and Christianity, or whether it was essentially determined by its Arabian ethos. Why set these two views over against each other instead of emphasizing their complementary aspects? It is clear that the new community came into direct conflict with some of the main religious traditions in pre-Islamic Arabia. The Qur'an itself echoes the resistance encountered by the preaching of the new faith that was so closely related to the Bible: the pagans protested against the affirmation of the unity of God and the resurrection of the body. And some of the moral demands for justice, reminding the affluent Meccan merchants that their wealth carried with it certain duties, set many of the rich against the new faith. Did not the people of the prophet Shu'ayb use the same words of reproach to their prophet that Muhammad heard in Mecca?

'Does thy prayer command thee that we should forsake what our fathers worshipped, or that we should not do what we will with our property?' (Qur'an 11.87).

On the other hand, in many ways the new movement responded to the aspirations of the Arab soul, with its sense of solidarity, generous hospitality, courage, military virtues, strong propensity for trade and travel with the attendant risk and profit, and the combination of alternating effort and ease. It was a religion that was close to nature, as the Qur'an itself says (Qur'an 30.30). In the same way, a great many pre-Islamic customs, like the pilgrimage to the sacred places of Mecca and its environs and the veneration of the Arabic language and eloquence, were retained after being purified of everything that linked them closely or remotely to the old polytheism.

The Qur'an itself emphasizes its Arabian side, and it certainly seems that at the beginning it offered itself as the Arabian expression of the eternal religion, the same religion that the Torah conveyed to the people of Moses and the Gospel to the people of Jesus. At one point it explains that God revealed the Qur'an to the Arabs so that they would not have an inferiority complex in relation to the older communities (those of the Jews and Christians, the commentators explain) and would not say:

'The Book was sent down only to two peoples before us, and we were indeed unaware of what they read' (Qur'an 6.156).

In a sense the Qur'an gave the Arabs the religious pride they lacked in the face of a certain arrogance on the part of the more advanced countries that surrounded them and had formerly established cordons of auxiliaries on their frontiers to prevent nomadic encroachments. With the Qur'an, the Muslim community was on an equal footing with the Jews and Christians, as it awaited the time that was coming to proclaim its universal mission.

The community was first formed in Mecca, where it was exposed to the hostility of the pagans. The Qur'an does not provide a coherent account of life at that time. The traditions tell us that certain passages were proclaimed on this or that occasion.Thus it is said that the Sura of Mary (Qur'an 19) was recited before the Negus by Muslims whom Muhammad had sent to Abyssinia to escape the persecution of the pagan Meccans. The texts of the Qur'an from this period provide rules of individual conduct and appeal to the virtues of gratitude and patience, referring to a body of laws that are reminiscent of the Decalogue (cf. Qur'an 17.23–38). There is a description of the first Muslims (cf. Qur'an 25.63–76). Doctrine is taught. The Muslims pray long into the night. Ritual is determined. All these elements are found in the so-called Meccan suras that date from before the year 622.

The text says little about Muhammad himself, except to report the famous journey that carried him to heaven (Qur'an 17.1) or to encourage him in his trials when his own people rejected him and the new community was boycotted by the pagan Meccans:

'Yet perhaps, if they believe not in this message, thou wilt torment thyself to death with grief over them' (Qur'an 18.6), says the text, referring to those who turn away when the Qur'an is proclaimed.

Elsewhere a kind of coexistence is advocated in so far as this attitude is the best suited to the circumstances:

'To you your religion, and to me my religion!' (Qur'an 109.6).

The community gradually took shape through testing times that gave it solidarity. Khadija, Muhammad's first wife, and Abu Bakr, his earliest companion who would succeed him as head of the community, put their wealth at the disposal of all those who were in difficulties due to persecution. The verses on almsgiving and generosity, as well as the condemnation of the wicked rich, must also be viewed in this context of solidarity.

There is no mention of international events, with one exception. It was at a time when the conflict between Byzantium and the Persians intensified. Jerusalem was taken by the Persians in 614 and retaken by Byzantium fourteen years later. A verse refers to a defeat of Byzantium and expresses the hope that a final victory will wipe out this reverse (Qur'an 30.1). In this connection, the commentator Baydawi recalls what the pagan Meccans said to the first Muslims. The Muslims' sympathy was with the Christians, while the pagans' was with Persia.

'You and the Byzantines,' they said to the Muslims, 'are People of the Book. We and the Persians are people without a Book.'

The exodus in 622 (the Hijra) marked a turning point in the life of the community. The Arab state, the seed from which the Arab-Muslim empire emerged, was born. Legislation was formulated, with regulations chiefly concerning matters of personal status (marriage, inheritance), contracts, holy war and booty, together with some prohibitions and the punishments prescribed for those who infringed them, and so on. These questions are too sensitive and call for too many fine distinctions to be treated in a few lines: it is enough to point to their existence. But the Qur'an increasingly emphasizes the necessity for taking the revealed texts as a basis for legislation.

'Whoso judges not by what God has sent down – they are the unbelievers' (Qur'an 5.47).

From the time of the Hijra, the Muslims increasingly stick together. They are reminded that they are all brothers. They are commanded not to associate unreservedly with non-Muslims. In places where the power of the community makes it possible, they are not to accept a non-Muslim leader at their head. The Muslim must take neither Jew nor Christian as a friend (Qur'an 5.51). The limits of association are ill-defined; it is only clear that they are not to consider non-Muslims as fully-fledged members of their political and religious brotherhood. Nor are they to treat them as confidants to whom they can say anything (Qur'an 3.118). Only another Muslim can be accepted without inhibition as the confidant of a Muslim.

However, this does not mean that social relations, even close ones, cannot be established between Muslims and non-Muslims.

'God does not forbid you, as regards those who have not fought against you on account of religion, nor driven you forth from your homes, that you should show them kindness, and deal justly with them; for God loves the just. God only forbids you those who have fought against you on account of religion, and have driven you forth from your homes, and have helped to drive you forth, that you should take them for friends. And

whosoever takes them for friends – these are the wrong-doers'
(Qur'an 60.8–9).

In Medina, living a common life drew the Muslims together.
The Arabs in the oasis who did not profess Judaism came over in
great numbers; some few were only nominally converted and sat
on the fence waiting to see how things would turn out. They are
called the 'hypocrites' and constitute a group that is sometimes
mentioned in the Qur'an. The others set to work, with Muhammad at their head, to build the mosque in Medina that became
the personal home of Muhammad and his wives as well as the
headquarters of the new state and the place for communal
prayer. Worship, religious observances and war strengthened
the bonds that united them. Ritual prayer held at the same
times, with everyone facing the same point, which soon became
the Ka'ba in Mecca, played an important part in preserving their
unity. Congregational prayer on Friday at noon, with the
gathering of almost all the men at the mosque, completed this
effect (cf. Qur'an 62.9–11). The fast at Ramadan and the annual
pilgrimage to Mecca were observed by the whole community.
Holy war created the solidarity of old soldiers among the first
Muslims. The customs of the desert had fostered a spirit of
independence. We observe them expressing their opinions on
several occasions. The Qur'an sanctions this approach, reminding Muhammad that he must consult his co-religionists on
important matters (Qur'an 42.38; 3.159).

The early years in Medina were physically hard and there was
great poverty. Therefore the razzias [raids] were both a means of
taking on the enemy and of procuring the necessities of life. The
Qur'an recalls several times that the Muslims had been morally
compelled to flee from Mecca because of persecution and that
they only sought to recover what they had lost. This they did first
by recourse to arms and then by negotiation.

The community did not allow itself to be victimized. It reacted
as soon as it could to assert its rights. And the Qur'an says clearly

that to put pressure on a Muslim to make him lose his faith is much more serious than to kill him. Therefore war is justifiable if it is necessary in order to put an end to these trials. The Qur'an contains a whole series of references to the raids that established the power of Islam. It mentions the Battle of Badr, the first victory of the Muslims in 624 (Qur'an 3.123), and expatiates on the questions that arose at that time: God's help, booty and the duty to take up arms (cf. the whole of Sura 8). It also recalls many other events.

Finally, Islam's mission is clearly expressed in a text that appears a number of times in the Qur'an; it concerns God's sending of Muhammad.

'It is He who has sent His Messenger with the guidance and the religion of truth, that He may cause it to prevail over all religion, though the idolaters be averse' (Qur'an 9.33).

The Muslims' cohesion is referred to on several occasions. It is described as a grace from God, since man would have been unable to achieve it by his own efforts alone. With a pride that challenges the money-grubbers who believe that everything can be bought, a text about Muslims proclaims:

God 'has brought their hearts together. Hadst thou expended all that is in the earth, thou couldst not have brought their hearts together; but God has brought their hearts together; surely He is Mighty, Wise' (Qur'an 8.63).

The new community also had to take a stand towards the Jews and Christians. The latter seem to have been thin on the ground in Mecca. There were some slaves, freedmen, foreign merchants and perhaps even a few soldiers, with an occasional itinerant preacher or monk encountered on a journey or in the town. This whole disparate group existed and the chronicles, like the commentators of the Qur'an, provide occasional details about them. However, a small circle seems to have had closer ties with Islam in its early days; we have referred to them above. There was Waraqa ibn Nawfal, the cousin of Khadija, Muhammad's first wife; some others are mentioned in addition to Waraqa.

The Muslims were few in number at that time and, as the commentators emphasize, God neither permitted nor asked them to use force then as they were to do in Medina after this verse gave them the green light to go to war:

'Sanction is given to those who fight because they were wronged – surely God is able to help them – who were driven forth from their homes without justification, only because they say "Our Lord is God"' (Qur'an 22.39–40).

And Jalalain's commentary notes that this verse is the first that was revealed on the subject of holy war.

In Mecca, the Qur'an calls for them to dispute with the People of the Book (that is, above all, the Jews and Christians) in the better way. Certain verses also recommend that, as a general rule, they choose the better means of persuasion:

'Not equal are the good deed and the evil deed. Repel evil with what is better and behold, he between whom and thee was enmity, shall be as if he were a warm friend' (Qur'an 41.34).

The word 'better', which recurs several times, is explained by Jalalain's commentary in the following way: repel evil by means of what is better, 'like anger with patience, ignorance with forbearance, offence with forgiveness'.

In Medina, after 622, the situation changed, for there there were many Jews, representing half the population of the oasis. A place as protected people had been reserved for them within the new political and religious state. Jealous of their independence, in their hearts they would not accept the restrictions on their freedom entailed by overtures and alliances; so they were eliminated. The Qur'an tells of the banishment of one of the tribes expelled from Medina and the distribution of their sequestered property (Qur'an 59.1–11). It also refers to the fate suffered by another tribe whose warriors were put to death for having attempted an ill-fated resistance while their women and children were sold as slaves (Qur'an 33.25–27).

A few dozen conversions took place among Jews and Christians in response to the advances of the new religion: they are mentioned several times (Qur'an 4.55; 46.10; 5.83). For those Christians and Jews determined to retain their religion, a place was provided in the Muslim polity on condition that they agreed to pay a poll tax and submitted to the Muslim political and cultural order. If they did not agree, it was decreed that force be used against them until they submitted:

'Fight against such of those who have been given the Book as believe not in God and the Last Day and do not forbid what God and His Messenger have forbidden, and practise not the religion of truth, until they pay the tribute [*jizya*] out of hand and have been humbled' (Qur'an 9.29).

The expression 'have been humbled' is explained in a work by the Pakistani Muslim leader Abul A'la Mawdudi in these terms: 'that is to say, they may not be "people in positions of power in this world", for these positions are reserved for Muslims only, because they perform the function of vicegerents of God'. And elsewhere, 'they are not in positions of power in the world, that is holders of the highest offices', which are reserved for Muslims alone.

These measures were actually applied in certain periods of history but they evolved in the course of time. The political and religious society of Islam lays claim to a legislation which is based on the Qur'an and the traditions but which, in reality, derives from a variety of sources, including the customs of the societies in which Islam took root in its early stages. The specifically Muslim aspect of these laws principally concerns general morality and personal status; the application of other measures depends on a whole series of factors that can only be dealt with by specialists.

The following text consists of commands and exhortations addressed to the community. It is taken from Sura 3, which is Medinan and dates from after the battles of Badr and Uhud; several verses refer to these in other places in the sura.

Commands and exhortations addressed to the community

99   Say: 'O People of the Book, why do you bar believers from the way of God, seeking to make it crooked, though you are witnesses? God is not heedless of the things you do.'

100   O believers, if you obey a party of those who have been given the Book, they will turn you, after you have believed, into unbelievers.

101   How can you disbelieve, when God's signs are recited to you and His Messenger is among you? Whoever holds fast to God, is already guided to a straight path.

102   O believers, fear God as He should be feared, and die not till you have surrendered [become Muslims].

103   And hold fast to the bond of God, all together, and do not separate; remember God's blessing upon you when you were enemies, and He brought your hearts together, so that by His blessing you became brothers. And you were on the brink of a pit of Fire, and He saved you from it. Thus does God make clear to you His signs, that you may be guided.

104 And let there be of you a community, inviting to good, enjoining what is right, and forbidding what is wrong; such are the prosperous.

105 Be not as those who separated and fell into dispute after the clear signs came to them; for them is a mighty chastisement.

110 You are the best community ever brought forth for mankind, enjoining what is right, forbidding what is wrong, and believing in God. If the People of the Book had believed, it would have been better for them; some of them are believers, but most of them are evil-doers (Qur'an 3.99–105, 110).

The verses translated above come from a much longer passage. They must not be regarded as a coherent whole; rather they suggest a recording taken in the course of a long exhortation, verging at times on a diatribe, to Muslims, Jews and Christians.

The term 'People of the Book' generally refers to Jews, Christians and groups affiliated with them. Here in Medina the interlocutors can only be the Jews of the oasis, who were opposed to Islam and refused to submit to a system of protectorate. The text accuses them of wanting to make Muslims lapse by converting them (see, too, Qur'an 2.109). The Muslim community has always defended itself vigorously against the dangers of apostasy. Verses like these foster vigilance among the faithful. The expression 'crooked way' appears several times in the Qur'an; it is contrasted with the 'straight way' commended by Islam. God's watchfulness that nothing escapes is also a frequent theme.

After challenging those who plot against Islam, the text addresses itself to Muslims to warn them against the danger of disloyalty.

'O believers' (verse 100) refers to Muslims, for faith in the Qur'an is synonymous with the Muslim faith. As is so often the case, the best way to inspire men's loyalty is to remind them of the benefits they have received. Thus verse 101 invokes the Qur'an and the person of Muhammad in order to confirm Muslims in their vocation. In fact, for the Muslim, the Qur'an (together with nature and miracles, one of the great 'signs' of God) is God's supreme gift to mankind. Over and above the details of its teaching, its very existence shows the extent of God's mercy towards men. Hence the flood of memories this simple phrase evokes in the believer.

As for the reference to the Messenger, Muhammad, who is among them, his impact on the faithful is equally great. Theoretically, in Islam, the revealed Book takes precedence over the Messenger, for the Book comes from heaven, a fully constituted whole, and the Messenger has only to transmit it. But in practice devotion to Muhammad is so deeply embedded in the emotional life of Muslims that an appeal like the one in this verse arouses profound emotions.

In Medina the Qur'an speaks of Muhammad more than it does in Mecca, referring to the opposition he encountered and even some details of his private life. Difficulties in the harem (cf. Qur'an 66.1–5), matrimonial problems and details of the etiquette to be observed when visiting him at the end of his life are mentioned (cf. Qur'an 33, passim). He is the Messenger of God and the seal of the prophets (cf. Qur'an 33.40). God and His angels bend down to bless him, and a verse that Muslims constantly repeat, on all occasions in life, calls down on him God's blessings and peace (Qur'an 33.56).

To return to our text. In verse 101, the phrase 'holds fast', or seeks security with God, expresses the bond that should exist between God and believers. The straight way appears here as a response to the crooked way in the preceding verse.

Verse 102 stresses the fear of God that is so often commended in the Qur'an. The simple phrase about death in the Muslim faith suggests an atmosphere of threats and damnation. He who does not die in submission to the one God has committed the great unforgiveable sin and faces an alarming future. This has led to the custom of repeating the testimony of faith over and over again before death, and when weakness at the end prevents the believer from speaking, his family hold up his arm with the forefinger pointing to the sky, to affirm to everyone his wish to die in the faith of the one God: one like the finger pointing heavenward.

Verse 103 alludes to the Muslims' unity. This unity was not easy. It was disrupted on several occasions even in Muhammad's lifetime and especially twenty-five years after his death, at the time of a terrible civil war that tore the community apart. Nevertheless, compared to the frequent inter-tribal wars, the Muslims' unity in the face of their pagan enemies impressed contemporaries. The Arabs, with their sensitive pride and their razzias, were not used to it. Muslim brotherhood represented a reality that often suffered reverses but could be appealed to by everyone in certain well-defined circumstances.

Verse 104 refers to the Muslim's mission in society and his struggle for the good. Many activist groups like the Muslim Brotherhood have advanced this verse to justify their moralistic interventions in a society they sought to reform.

Having omitted several verses, we have finally reproduced verse 110. Of all the verses in the Qur'an, the first phrase in this verse is perhaps the one most frequently cited by preachers. It is written in huge letters in the magnificent meeting hall of the Palace of the Arab League in Cairo. It justifies Muslim pride and the consciousness of being the 'best' in this world. It is the counterpart of the phrase 'You are the salt of the earth,' addressed by Jesus to his followers in the Sermon on the Mount.

And finally the text comes back to the People of the Book, the Jews and Christians, to regret that most of them have remained deaf to the appeals of Islam. If they had believed, it would have been better for them. And the text renews the reproach that they are divided, a reproach that plays such a large part in the Muslim vision of the world. For Islam, Christians and Jews, instead of forming one community, are split up, with each group excommunicating its neighbour, and this after having refused to accept the revealed truth. The Qur'an was a call to recover unity in the bosom of Islam: they rejected it. On the Last Day God will make known to them the reason for their divisions.

The Muslim community is made up not only of humans; it also includes angels and jinn. Angels, whose existence is an article of faith, sing God's praises and implore His forgiveness for earthly creatures (Qur'an 42.5). Others perform various functions in the service of God.

Jinn, beings created from fire (cf. Qur'an 15.27), form a special category in which there are Muslim jinn and unbelieving jinn. They were moved by the preaching of the Qur'an (cf. Qur'an 46.29–32) and some of them believed (cf. Qur'an 72, passim). Their relations with the Muslim community are not altogether clear. Until recently, especially in female circles, life was lived in intimate contact with the jinn, who were feared and placated. It is probable that this aspect of doctrine facilitated the adoption of Islam by many animist peoples in Africa and elsewhere who were accustomed to spirit worship. The Muslim community is not composed solely of human beings.

The community also transcends earthly existence. A day will come when God will restore life to the dead, who will rise again. On that day everyone will be judged and the good will go to the paradise that is promised to the faithful. True Muslims will all meet again in this garden of delights. Believers hope, too, that on the Day of Judgment the weight of their sins placed on one of the scales of the balance will be less than that of their good deeds on the othere scale:

'Good deeds drive away evil deeds' (Qur'an 11.114).

There are a number of texts in the Qur'an which describe the upheavals at the end of the world (cf. Qur'an 81.1–14) and especially paradise and hell, with the sins that lead to the latter and the good deeds that preserve one from it. It is difficult to appreciate these passages when one's feelings have not been moulded from childhood. The descriptions of the joys of paradise, food, drink, shade, greetings of peace and the houris, the heavenly beauties created for men's ease, stand in contrast to the torments endured by the damned. Some Muslims take these descriptions in a symbolic rather than a strict sense. The majority adhere to the literal meaning, aware at the same time that there is a gulf between the realities of this world and the next.

At all events, the high point of emotion in paradise will be the mutual satisfaction of the divine Lord and His servant. The latter is happy and has all he could wish for: God is satisfied with him. This idea appears in some famous verses. It is said that Rabi'a, the Muslim woman mystic who lived in the eighth century in Basra, heard a voice reciting this text as her death approached:

> 'O soul at peace return unto thy Lord
> Well pleased and pleasing Him!
> Enter thou among My servants!
> Enter thou My Paradise!'
>
> (Qur'an 89.27–30).

9

Argument and Persuasion

The message conveyed by a book affects the reader as much by its form as by its content. When Muslims flock round a reciter of the Qur'an to hear him slowly chant the verses, it is certainly because of the doctrinal content of a text that leads to reflection. Could it not also be as much, or even more, due to the style, the rhythm and the music of the phrases and words as to the quality of the exposition? And so, having had a good look at the ideas, we will conclude this study with some reflections on the Qur'an's mode of argument and persuasion. A last glance will perhaps help to deepen our understanding of the hold it exercises over believers.

It is certainly not by chance that the apologetic aspect of the Qur'an is highly developed. This was an effect of the atmosphere surrounding Islam's origins: Muhammad was impugned by his entourage and even by his next of kin. The pagans bombarded him with objections directed at his own person and did not accept him as a prophet. After the Hijra in 622, this opposition turned into war. In the same period, after a few months of expectancy and vain attempts to win over the Jewish tribes of the oasis, the position of the Muslims in Medina hardened: once again there was recourse to arms. At the same time, the bedouins and those who had only nominally converted continued to make things difficult for the genuine Muslims who had given themselves body and soul to the new religion. In short, the Qur'an is continually called upon to respond to critics and to condemn opponents. Its way of dealing with these burning questions always has a quality of immediacy and something striking and appealing about it. It is said that the future Caliph 'Umar, who came as a fierce pagan to plague the nascent community, ended up, like St Paul on the road to Damascus, convinced, converted and shaken to the core, after he heard the chanting of a Qur'anic text that completely transformed him.

This feature of argument and persuasion appears continually in the Qur'an. It is rare that long passages do not include, as parenthetical phrases, an interrogation, an apologetic allusion, an exhortation or a rebuke. The discourse does not take place in the abstract: it is a far cry from an academic lecture given to an audience that is frozen in its seats. On the contrary, as in some popular literary genres (or modern avant-garde ones), readers are repeatedly challenged to come to a decision and to affirm their faith in what the Qur'an offers them, in short to join the believers' camp and flee, without delay, the camp of the opposition. In the course of the preceding pages, various techniques of style and exposition have been considered. It is now time to return to this subject. A few examples will suffice to draw attention to a topic which deserves to be treated independently and which Arab religious criticism has long addressed.

The first point that strikes the reader is the simplicity of the Qur'anic arguments and also their vivid, concrete character. For example, the Qur'an continually returns to the affirmation that God is one and has no equal or associate. To fix this truth firmly in the hearts and minds of the faithful, the Qur'an appeals to their experience. They are well aware that pagan Arabs before Islam admitted only one creator God into their pantheon: they called him Allah. The Qur'an makes them repeat it:

'If thou askest them, "Who created the heavens and the earth?," they will surely say, "Allah" (God)' (Qur'an 39.39).

Hence the Qur'an emphasizes the impotence of other gods

who are incapable of creating even a fly, providing benefits or opposing the decisions of the creator God. If they are so powerless and incapable, what good is it to treat them as gods and believe in them?

Elsewhere, to ridicule the pagans' pantheon, the Qur'an relies on the down-to-earth popular good sense of men in Arabia. They admit the existence of female deities, while in everyday life they look down on women from their position of male superiority: does not an Arab frown at the announcement of the birth of a girl when he very much hoped for a boy? They why do they attribute to God what they do not want for themselves (cf. Qur'an 43.16–18)?

The Qur'an goes further: it expresses in picturesque terms an argument that is found in the works of philosophers. The unity of the world is proof of the unity of the principle from which it derives its origin: it is proof of the unity of the Creator. If one looks closely at the following argument, it is clear that the image does not fall short of the thought, far from it.

'God has not taken to Himself any son, nor is there any god with Him; for then each god would have taken away that which he had created and some of them would have risen up over others' (Qur'an 23.91).

Starting from a commonplace conflict in this world, the rivalry of owners, each of whom clings to his own property, the Qur'an passes to the opposite idea, the absence of rivalry that proves that the Lord of the world is one.

This attack on the pantheons, coupled with another attack on divine generation conceived in human terms, is conducted relentlessly. The text sometimes speaks ironically as it stresses the absence of sexuality in God: God has no children because He has no wives.

These extremely simple arguments are constantly repeated by Muslims. They are directly bound up with their view of God, the

Creator and Lord of the universe. There is no hiatus between their doctrine, their daily experience and their liturgy. Like slogans which, once heard, keep coming back to mind, the pronouncements in the Qur'an are known by everyone and repeated whenever there is cause to justify the faith.

This simplification is effective in reducing primitive paganism to silence. It is equally effective in the face of neo-paganisms like the deification of material things, money and the state.

The same simplification is also found in the attitude to Christianity. In the Qur'an, Jesus declares categorically that he never told men to regard himself and his mother as two deities associated with the one God. Those who worship the triad God–Mary–Jesus are confuted. To whom is this rebuke addressed? The Qur'an does not specify, and Christians for their part do not feel that it concerns them. It has been noted that, according to the authors of heresiologies, a group called the Collyridians worshipped this triad. Could the rebuke be aimed at them? A similar simplification occurs in the formulation of another proposition. To say that 'God is the Messiah', as if the whole divine mystery came down to the blasphemous deification of a man, is described by the Qur'an as flagrant impiety.

Christians have often remarked that the dogma of the church has quite different connotations and does not tally with the offending expressions. They think that the Qur'an was directed at misrepresentations of Christianity that are also rejected by the church.

Together with the simplicity of its images and arguments or, if you prefer, its concrete character, another feature of Qur'anic apologetic is to seek to arouse admiration and fear by the frequent evocation of God's omnipotence. God's omnipotence is revealed in creation, cosmic phenomena, the births that the Qur'an so often mentions, in wind and in the rain that restores life to the parched deserts: there can be no objection to this. Such thoughts strengthen the faith of the faithful and remind them of an aspect of God's majesty.

Furthermore, this same omnipotence is put forward to reaffirm that nothing is impossible for God. To the Muslim, the credibility of doctrines like the resurrection of the dead or the triumph of the prophets is not at all extraordinary when viewed from this perspective. God can do anything.

Thus, taking up a traditional argument that figures in rabbinic literature as well as in works of the church fathers, the Qur'an explains that God, having created man the first time, is capable of recreating him a second time by raising him from the dead (cf. Qur'an 22.5, among others). The same argument already appears in the Bible, put into the mouth of the mother of the seven martyrs, when she exhorts her sons, assuring them that God will restore a life offered for Him:

'I do not know how you appeared in my womb; it was not I who endowed you with breath and life, I had not the shaping of your every part. It is the creator of the world, ordaining the process of man's birth and presiding over the origin of all things, who in His mercy will most surely give you back both breath and life' (II Maccabees 7.22–23).

In the same way, the inevitability of divine retribution on the day of the Last Judgment, a day when divine omnipotence will recompense the good and chasten the wicked, is there to make man understand that he cannot escape God and that all rebellion will be punished. The example of the destruction of the people who did not obey the Messengers sent by God recurs over and over again in the Qur'an as a warning to those who do not toe the line. The omnipotence of God that unleashed the Flood, razed Sodom and Gomorrah and engulfed Pharaoh in the Red Sea, will descend upon the guilty on the Day of Judgment. In addition to reasons intended to convince those who questioned mono-theism, there are threats and fear. The range of emotions evoked is extended: the fire awaits not only the polytheist and the man who refuses to believe in the prophets but also the selfish and the wicked rich.

While the Qur'an's influence owes much to its simplicity and its concreteness, as it does to the reminder of God's omnipotence, the role it plays in the Muslim experience of the divine must not be forgotten. It is by the Qur'an and through the Qur'an that the faithful come to a knowledge of God and an awareness of His presence: in particular it develops the sense of the sacred. In actual fact the word sacred itself only appears very rarely in the Qur'an, in connection with the liturgy, observances, prayer and places, but the reality it represents is there. It is especially in the words 'of God' that the notion of the sacred is most often expressed. The Qur'an is not called a sacred book but it is called the book of God. The Ka'ba is sometimes designated by the term sacred temple (or house), but it is also called, more simply, the temple or house of God. A sacred territory is a land of God. Creatures are 'signs of God', and even when it comes to an ancient form of the sacred in Arabia, it is said to be the 'camel of God' to denote a sacred camel.

The sacred is the mark imprinted by God on the realities of this life by the very fact of their being in direct contact, temporary or permanent, with Him, thus helping man in his experience of the divine, whether in worship, praise, thanksgiving, vows, and so on. Over and above the realities that God has declared sacred, everything can be sanctified. The Muslim does not confuse what must not be confused: God alone is God. But as everything was created by Him, He is present everywhere, in everything; He sees all and protects in such a way that no one can resist His protection. The enormous influence exerted by the Qur'an is due, in large measure, to the sense of God's presence that it fosters, as well as the respect for God's signs in creation, to which it calls attention.

So far in these reflections on argument and persuasion, we have remained on ground that is common to all the monotheistic religions. Indeed, in many respects Muslim apologetic has

resembled certain Jewish or Christian apologetics. In the face of
the surrounding paganism, Islam sided with the biblical religions
that also believe in one God and the resurrection of the dead,
doctrines rejected by the pagan Arabs. It is not surprising that
the same doctrines were defended by similar arguments.

On the other hand, when it proclaimed that Judaism and
Christianity had been corrupted and that it had come to restore
the true religion in all its purity, Islam was in conflict with them.
Hence there is a second order of apologetic arguments intended
to establish the authenticity of Muhammad's prophetic mission
and therefore of the Qur'an itself. The examples selected will
consequently be much more distinctive. The rhythm of the style
and the implication of the pronouncements need to be carefully
considered. It will be useful to outline the profound psychological forces brought into play by the argument.

First, having just noted the concern for simplicity and the
concreteness of the examples that characterized the first
arguments, it is now time to point to the emotional dimension of
the discourse. The logic is steeped in feeling and at times the
intensity of emotion is revealed by a disruption in the thread of
the argument.

To take an example: 'A'isha, the Prophet's youngest wife,
after a minor incident that left her alone in the desert (she went
to look for a necklace that she had lost), had to make her own
way back to the camp. A young bedouin who was there by
chance accompanied her: this gave rise to a series of often quite
malicious comments that deeply divided the community. Some
talked of adultery, others believed 'A'isha to be innocent.
Muhammad was very troubled. He hesitated for some weeks,
wondering whether or not he ought to repudiate his favourite
wife. Finally a revelation took place that declared her innocent.
And the Qur'an, recalling that every accusation against a
woman's honour must be supported by the evidence of four
responsible men, adds, concerning the accusers:

'Why did they not bring four witnesses to prove it? But since they did not bring the witnesses, in the sight of God they are liars' (Qur'an 24.13).

The rhetorical effect is due to the fact that the conclusion goes beyond the premises. An undercurrent of indignation runs through the sentence. Strictly speaking, it should say: if they have not produced four witnesses, their demand is legally inadmissable. The absence of witnesses takes place on the legal plane without taking account of the realities of the situation. How could these four witnesses be found in the solitude of the desert? But the infectious indignation upsets the logic of the style: the transition from legality to reality betrays the depth of the emotion. The epithet 'liar' seems to have been proved by the foregoing, whereas in fact there is a break in the thread of the argument. The faithful who believe in the divine origin of the text will accept that the spiteful gossips in question are liars, in the name of the sacred character of the Qur'an that says so. People of goodwill will think the same thing without being able to prove it. If one weighs the words dispassionately, one can only conclude that this is an outburst of eloquence that conceals the impossibility of knowing anything, and end up shelving the matter. And yet, the pitiless word 'liar', the last word in the verse, will stick in the mind to disturb the reader's subconscious. The Qur'an's persuasive power is inseparable from its literary devices.

The same emotion is found again in the accusations made by the unbelievers against Muhammad and the Qur'an. There are several references in the Qur'an to complaints that Muhammad composed it himself with the help of informants (cf. Qur'an 25.4–5), or even, according to some, that another person was the author of the text. Elsewhere he is regarded as a poet, a soothsayer or possessed by jinn: that is, he is classed with the authors of oracles who were suspected of being in touch with occult powers. But the text goes on at once, by way of refutation, to put these words into God's mouth:

'If he had invented concerning Us any sayings, We would surely have seized him by the right hand, and then cut his life-vein and not one of you could have defended him' (Qur'an 69.44–46).

The effect produced on the listener is immediate. While in the same sura, a few verses above, the text is content solemnly to declare the divine origin of the Qur'an, here it has God Himself intervene, employing the conditional 'if', several usages of which have already been noted. Calm prevails, Muhammad continues his activity. But the word 'if' gives this calm a dramatic depth. If Muhammad had lied, attributing to God words that were not God's, he would have been punished immediately. The fact that no catastrophe has taken place becomes proof of the Qur'an's authenticity.

It should be noted that the text avoids using a hard word like 'lie' or any other that, imprinted on the memory of believers and linked with the idea of Muhammad's message, could have an undermining effect. There are merely words with pejorative overtones. On the other hand, it authoritatively affirms the conditional punishment that would follow. An assertion of this kind has a powerful impact. The image of immediate death and spurting blood makes the flesh creep . . . The argument is very compelling when one already believes in the divine origin of the Qur'an. It does not actually prove anything, but for those who already have faith it strengthens them in that faith. For, in strict logic, given that God has refrained and refrains from intervening in the experience of hundreds of religious leaders and others, and does not intervene before the end, the threat is not consistent with the way God usually acts. We are in the realm of pure faith, not of rational proof.

The argument takes a more rational turn in a small number of very important cases. The attacks on Muhammad's sincerity seem to have been, if not multiplied, at least made explicit as the years went by in Mecca. In the period that preceded the Hijra, a rumour circulated: he was taught, they said, by another person whose name was given. The origin of the Qur'an, according to opponents, was not what it claimed. The sura of the Bee (Sura 16) states the objection and immediately responds to it:

'And We know very well that they say: "It is only a mortal who teaches him." But the speech of him they hint at is foreign, while this is Arabic speech, clear' (Qur'an 16.103).

Let us examine this verse: briefly and succinctly the Qur'an reports an objection. The simple reminder is a way of saying that the opposition is known, thus letting it be understood that it does not occasion fear or dismay. In a similar fashion, heads of state refer in their speeches to what is said against them before refuting it.

The objection is always the same. Muhammad, say his enemies, had help in composing the Qur'an. Yet the text remains extremely general, perhaps so as not to make an unfavourable impression on the faithful. When reporting objections, one always has to avoid presenting them too forcefully, lest the audience is rendered unresponsive to refutations. The effect obtained would then be contrary to the desired aim. Here nothing is said about the way in which Muhammad is accused of being taught. Is he accused of receiving a complete text that he repeats, or rather of receiving information that enriches his subconscious? It is impossible to say. One only notes that the accusation explicitly mentions a particular well-known informant, whereas the earliest suras spoke of several aids or informants (cf. Qur'an 25.4 among others).

As soon as it has stated the objection, the Qur'an replies with well-chosen words. The expression 'him they hint at' is pejorative, implying a species of corruption. Today a word with this root serves to denote atheists and dissidents. Thus the very choice of the verb puts us on our guard against this man. The argument is clear: the man's mother tongue is not Arabic, therefore he cannot be the author of a book that is written in beautiful Arabic. At this point Muslim commentators provide the names of a number of people in Mecca, generally slaves or Christian freedmen, who had a good knowledge of the Jewish and Christian sacred books.

It is the first time that such a clear argument appears. It thus rules out all the assertions that view the Qur'an as the work of a contemporary that Muhammad learned and repeated. Once again, the statement rightly focuses on the fact that a non-Arab would be utterly incapable of composing a text like the Qur'an. However, the reply takes no notice at all of another aspect of the question: did these contemporaries tell Muhammad, even in bad Arabic, stories of the Ancients that he knew nothing about and that the Qur'an then repeated? A logical examination of the verse forces us to answer that the text says nothing about the subject. One can only conclude that there were in Mecca at that time a small number of persons who knew these old stories and that Muhammad was in contact with them. If these people had not existed, the objection would have had no weight and would have fallen away of its own accord.

The polemic between the first Muslims and their enemies must have been closely argued, and only the final victory enabled the primitive community to gain credence. The situation is easy to imagine. Opponents asked Muhammad for a miracle (a sign, to use the Qur'anic expression) that would be an indisputable token of his mission, and they added that the former prophets had all proved the authenticity of their mission by such wonders. The Qur'an does not reply immediately: at times it even implies that signs would be useless in the case of people who are ill disposed. Then, in the years that preceded the Hijra, its position became clear. It remains for us to examine the arguments that were then put forward. This will be our last example. Today, when Muslims want to prove the divine origin of the Qur'an, they still go back to the same line of reasoning.

Everything revolves around a notion that Muslim theology characterizes by one word, 'the challenge'. The Qur'an challenges anyone, be he man or jinn, even if they help each other, to compose something that resembles the Qur'an. The formulation of the challenge was elaborated. At the beginning, the principle alone was stated (cf. Qur'an 17.88); but the texts soon clarified the conditions of this ordeal. Opponents were asked to try to write ten suras (Qur'an 11.13), or even only one (Qur'an 10.38), comparable to those in the Qur'an. If they did not succeed, it would be proof that the Qur'an comes from God.

'And if you are in doubt about what We have sent down to Our servant, then produce a sura like it, and call your witnesses, beside God, if you are truthful' (Qur'an 2.23).

From that time onwards, the question has been regularly studied in Muslim theology. All students learn the names of the would-be prophets who tried to take up the challenge and failed in the attempt. Some Muslim thinkers, however, have observed that it would not be difficult to imitate one of the shorter suras at the end of the Qur'anic corpus. But they immediately add: if no one has succeeded, it is because God has positively prevented those who wished to try. And the jurists have systematically distinguished two cases. Either it is physically impossible for a creature to compose a single sura, or else it would be physically possible to do so, but God has positively prevented those who would be inclined to embark on such a venture.

What has been the fate of this argument? Considered irrefutable by Muslims, it has been contested by those who do not share their faith. Non-Muslims consider that it proves nothing. There are sufficient human reasons, they say, for a book not to be imitated (in the first place, the unique, distinctive character of every work of art or, if you prefer, the unique, distinctive character of every author, who is nurtured emotionally and spiritually in a particular fashion and placed by life in circumstances in which no one else has been placed in exactly the same way). There is no need to have recourse to supernatural reasons. But to enter into this kind of discussion would be to go outside the scope of the present work, which is intended only to facilitate a first encounter with the Qur'an.

Conclusion

The survey that we have undertaken remains intentionally brief. Our first purpose has been to become familiar with the great themes that are developed in the Qur'an and also with some of its literary devices. Other problems will very soon arise. We have touched on some of them. Before addressing them, it is necessary to read the texts seriously and to understand them. It is now up to readers to continue the work, alone or with other help.

Two ways are open to them.

The first is that of the history of classic religions, with its concern to compare, to establish connections and to investigate origins or the affinities that exist between themes and texts. This way has its limitations but it remains irreplaceable. In the course of the preceding pages we have often adopted it, noting the things that draw us together and those that separate us. Thus we have found the sense of God the Creator and the grandeur of creation singing the praises of its author, a theme that is also present in the Old Testament, as it is in Christianity (think of St Francis of Assisi's Canticle of the Creatures). We have encountered fundamental religious values, with their openness to God, that are very similar for Christian and Muslim.

At the same time, this way is conducive to facing mutual reproaches and accusations squarely and attempting to see them clearly. In the end, one cannot avoid pointing to the essential differences between Christianity and Islam: a different sense of

the majesty of God, a different view of the way God ap-
proaches men, man's different attitude before the divine mystery, a different conception of man's vocation, whether he is
called to discipline himself in order to follow the straight way,
or to rise above himself and be transformed by baptism in the
Holy Spirit and adoption as children of God. All these
differences could be said to come down to one: the way in
which Christians and Muslims conceive of Christ and his role.
Or, to approach the problem from another angle, the question
of revelation: is the pinnacle of revelation realized in a sacred
book, like the Qur'an, or in a living person like Christ? All
these differences are originally theological problems, and
Christians' firm conviction that they are monotheists seems
incomprehensible to most Muslims, except for a minority. This
is without doubt because the divine mystery is beyond our
comprehension, but also perhaps because Christians themselves have not been sufficiently concerned to explain their
position.

The first way leads to historical research on the Scriptures
and the reliability of their testimony. And we are faced with
two points of view. On the one hand, there is the view of
Muslims, for whom the Qur'an alone is of consequence, given
the argument of the challenge and the fact that no one has ever
been able to compose a sura comparable to those of the
original. On the other hand, there is the view of Christians,
who regard this argument as invalid and, conscious of the
reliability of the transmission of the essential gospel message,
see no reason to question their faith. The fact that a number of
prophetic movements throughout history have harboured similar grievances against Christianity has enured them to this kind
of attack.

All the same, there is a danger that Christians and Muslims
may harden their respective postures and face each other in a
deadlock. A situation like this leads sooner or later to apologetic confrontations which are sometimes necessary, but which,

if not set in a proper perspective, run the risk of quickly stifling and killing all sympathy, openness and understanding of the other.

The second way open to readers of the Qur'an involves great tact and humility on their part. The horizons are no longer the same as in the standard history of religions. The old catechisms spoke of three distinct elements in human actions: matter, knowledge and consent. This was to remind us that the quality of actions is not to be found simply on the material level of choices and conduct. Historical and personal factors intervene to give these choices a different direction or consequence from what their material aspect would suggest. Taking the various existential factors into account, we therefore consider man first of all in the presence of his Creator with the relation that exists between them. The Qur'an plays an important part in the personal dialogue between each Muslim and his Creator, and the surrender to the will of God that Islam signifies is at the same time an openness to the mysterious gifts of God. This second type of reading will therefore concentrate on the existential relations between the believer and his Lord, seeking to discover how the Muslim is fortified by the Qur'an, which elements sustain him and which others inspire behaviour that is less easy for us to understand. By underscoring the main lines of Qur'anic teaching, the preceding pages will also, we hope, help readers to embark on this second way. The information found here is once again very brief, but it will point to subsequent discoveries. In the same way a guide or map can never take the place of a personal journey to a country but prepares for and facilitates it.

At all events, for the millions who profess Islam, the Qur'an has always represented, and still represents, an approach to God. It may be that, disconcerted by different sensibilities and social practices, readers will find it hard to appreciate the thoughts and the style. It may be, too, that, accustomed to a Christian approach to God, they will feel disorientated and experience an impression of emptiness, as they seek to discover the sense of human grandeur and misery, or the formation of the new creature by the Holy Spirit, that are so essential to Christian doctrine.

It is difficult to understand the fascination that the Qur'an exerts without mentally putting oneself in the place of the Muslim, who finds God when he recites it, looks to it for guiding principles, and for whom the Qur'an is the presence of God. Even minute descriptions of a region will remain incomplete if they do not allow for the light. In reality the most insignificant landscape takes on another aspect as soon as the colours glow in the sun, or when the rain, despite its brilliance as it falls, casts a pall over human beings and forms. A description of the Qur'an must reflect this light, which is the encounter with God.

Index of Qur'anic References

General Index